GALL

Overcoming the Power of Dominating Emotions

GALL

All Scriptures taken from the King James Bible
the Amplified® Bible , and the Message Bible
"Scripture quotations taken from the Amplified® Bible,
Copyright © 1954,1958, 1962, 1964, 1965, 1987 by The
Lockman Foundation Used by permission."
(www.lockman.org)
 "Scripture taken from *The Message*. Copyright © 1993, 1994, 1995, 1996,
2000, 2001, 2002. Used by permission of NavPress Publishing Group."

GALL Volume no.1 555 Media Publishing
©2014 All Rights Reserved
Reproduction/Duplication without expressed consent from
Richard Taylor/555 media strictly prohibited by applicable Laws

Table of Contents

1. Preface — 4
2. Introduction: Gall-The Poisoner of Purpose — 5
3. Fornicating with the Serpent — 9
4. Spiritual Immune Systems — 17
5. Dominating Emotions — 20
6. A Vesture Dipped in Blood — 25
7. The Procreative Mind — 31
8. Prepared for Battle — 39
9. Towers of Unbelief — 41
10. Refraining The Mouth — 51
11. Jesus was our Job — 56
12. Bitterness Pt 1 — 61
13. Bitterness Pt 2 (Cancelling Emotional Debts) — 74
14. Despising the Shame — 80
15. Rejection — 90
16. Pride and Corruption Part 1 — 99
17. Pride and Division Modern Day Corrupters — 104
18. Pride Again — 109
19. Self-Pity — 115
20. Fear: The Torment Trap — 120
21. The Dominion of Love — 128
22. Established in Peace — 135

Preface

I have heard the question asked, can a Believer have faith in the heart, and still struggle with dominating emotions in the mind or soul. The answer is absolutely YES?!

While many hold on to the promises of God in their hearts, most have yet to figure out an adequate defense against dominating emotions in the mind. For many, the mind has become an ungated community...

One encounter with Kingdom Truth can erect and securely lock the gate;...As Kingdom Truth increases in volume and revelation, the mindgate is gird with kingdom authority declaring "do not enter", "no trespassing", "no imaginations" and "God's property"...The Mind then becomes a gated community patrolled by peace.

Introduction
Gall- The Poisoner of Purpose

And when they were come unto a place called Golgotha, that is to say, a place of a skull, They gave him vinegar to drink mingled with gall: and when he had tasted thereof, he would not drink... **Matt 27:33-35**

Tempted Beyond Measure...

These soldiers had already beaten him beyond recognition (see Isaiah 52:13-14), crowned him with (spike-like) thorns, spat in his face, and mocked him repeatedly...He had tasted and submitted to more bitter suffering at the hands of demon inspired men than any other living being, yet he refused to drink the vinegar (sour wine) mixed with Gall (a bitter poisonous extract made from myrrh). Every other form of suffering was endurable, including the anguishing of his soul, the ripping away of his flesh, and the nailing of his body to the Cross. ***But there was one thing Jesus would not do...*He refused to <u>drink the gall</u> *(The Cup of Bitterness)*. THOUGHT:**

What life event has caused you great anguish of heart? An unfaithful spouse, the loss of a loved one, betrayal by a trusted friend, unfulfilled promises from someone you opened up your heart to, a health scare, a spiritual affliction, any one of a number of life events can begin the formation of a root of bitterness, shame, rejection, fear, pride or self-pity. These roots, if left unchecked and allowed to grow will eventually wrap themselves around the human soul and manifest as Dominating Emotions. **Note:** Our emotions were never intended to have dominion over us, but to be in subjection to the spirit of man, and to the Spirit of God. **Example:** Before Adam and Eve sinned, they were naked and not ashamed, after they sinned, they were *afraid* because they were naked, and they covered themselves with fig leaves (a sign of *shame*). This account in Genesis Chapter 3 gives us the first picture of Dominating Emotions.

The Epidemic Plague of Modern Times

Human pain, suffering, and anguish in these trying times has produced an epidemic harvest of bitterness and unforgiveness in the hearts of the masses. Demonic oppression and torment have assailed against mankind in cataclysmic proportion. Abuses, molestations, rejections, devastations, traumas, tests, trials, torments, snares, disappointments, rejections, betrayals, abandonments, adulteries, incest, battering and countless other afflictions in every arena of life often justify to the human soul "Drink the Cup…", "Drink the Cup…", "Drink the cup of Gall". All too often this happens without realizing it, even in the hearts of God's own people who have not guarded this precious place reserved unto God, and have unwittingly allowed the Serpent to gain entrance and have intimacy.

Justified anger never Justifies Bitterness

While the Cup of Bitterness may seem appealing to the eyes, BEWARE, it has a very nasty after taste, along with very harmful side effects. After his ejection from Heaven's doors, Satan himself came into the garden of Eden in the form of a Serpent, with a forked tongue, hissing... A "hiss", is defined as The Sound of Bitterness or Resentment. Like Jesus on the Cross, we must refuse to drink that cup, or we will eventually voice that "hiss"... Jesus had every right to be bitter, didn't he? Seems justified on the surface, doesn't it? But no! Bitterness bonds us with the affliction, the pain and the suffering..., We marry it!

Are you married to a life event from your past? Have you been altered in your identity by traumas and torments? Has it been difficult to accomplish the God given desires that are burning within your heart. Are you having difficulty sustaining close relationships? You may be suffering from the influence of a Dominating Emotion. The truth is that many people don't even know that they are being controlled by a Dominating Emotion that entered in through a past life event. Often, this occurs because they have, whether consciously or unconsciously, pushed that painful experience down into the undetectable realms of the soul [The Mind, Will, Intellect and Emotions]. Yes, there are places in the soul where "old pain" gets stored away for future resolution. We often do this as a "Survival Mechanism". The problem is that even underlying Dominating Emotions effect our personalities and steal our joy. I believe that this book represents for you, a "Divine Appointment" with your Healing, Deliverance and Life Event Resolution! Remember, whatever Dominating Emotion you detect as you read this book, this is a Huge Step towards reigniting your purpose, and realigning your destiny. The truth is that almost every negative life event or spiritual attack has a significant impact upon our emotions. This book presents truth for prevention, protection, inoculation, nutrition, healing, repentance and deliverance. It also reveals overcoming strategies, trusted tools, magnificent mysteries, liberating revelations, declarations, confessions, prayer points, undisclosed Kingdom truths, and overcoming testimonies. Chew Slowly, and Eat Well!

Fornicating with the Serpent

The First Time I heard the words "Fornicating with the Serpent" was in a Christian Assembly that I was serving in. ….One particular Sunday I sensed a familiar opposition coming from a person in the Church, only this time, it was heightened, and there was a contention in the realm of the Spirit concerning the Word I was assigned to deliver…As I proceeded, the opposition and hindrance became more volatile, then I received a Word of Knowledge saying *"Someone is Fornicating with the Serpent"*…I was aware, very aware of who it was, but chose not to expose them openly. Immediately after this, I was given the understanding of the message, and explained to the Church that when we entertain evil in our hearts (give place to iniquity), we are having an intimate encounter with the enemy of our souls. After speaking this out, there was a loud scream let out by a person in the meeting and the hindrance was immediately broken. In this case, the evil spirit left immediately when it was exposed to light (the revelation of fornicating with the serpent). ***Prayer:*** **Consume me Lord, that I never allow the Serpent to roam in the garden of my mind, or burrow down into the caverns of my heart…(Holy Spirit lead me through this prayer)** In other words, what we entertain in our minds and thoughts, can become a great seducer to our hearts and bodies.

Jesus taught us something on the glorious day of the crucifixion as demons groveled at His apparent defeat... He taught us that if we remain submitted (in mind and heart as knowing God's providential Love for us) to the Father, we can rule our souls in the midst of any trial, and overcome every kind of evil with good! This is especially needed for protection against spiritual, mental and emotional injury! The Idea here is that of submitting to God, and not standing on our own strength. Jesus could only effectively resist the devil, the Gall of Bitterness, by being submitted fully to God. **<u>DECLARE THIS WITH ME:</u>**

"I AM FULLY SUBMITTED TO GOD"

Submit yourselves therefore to God, resist the devil, and he will flee from you. **James 4:7**

Though there are many examples of Fornication with the Serpent in scripture, the most notable would be that of Judas Iscariot (The Disciple of Jesus).

He it is, to whom I shall give a sop, when I have dipped it. And when he had dipped the sop, he gave it to Judas Iscariot, the son of Simon. And after the sop **<u>Satan entered into him.</u>** *Then said Jesus unto him, That thou doest, do quickly.*

John 13:26-27

The two words in the original New Testament Greek for "entered into" are "eiserchomai" to enter and "eis" into. This is a double emphasis. This is the only scenario in all of Scripture where it is stated that Satan himself (and not a demon or evil spirit) entered into a person, clearly this entrance was deep and purposed. The statement, "Satan entered into him", could be understood as a figure of speech representing a demon or evil spirit, but given the assignment that Judas was recruited for, (to betray the Lord Jesus Christ) I believe that the Scripture can be interpreted literally. Judas had been carrying on a long term evil affair in the area of his thoughts and intentions, and because of this, his conscience became seared….

The Apostle Paul warns of this phenomenon: *Now the Spirit speaketh expressly, that in the latter times some shall depart from the faith,* **_giving heed to seducing spirits_**, *and doctrines of devils; Speaking lies in hypocrisy;* **_having their conscience seared with a hot iron;_** **1Timothy 4:1 –2**

You'll notice that the language in this verse depicts these seducing spirits as aggressors actively pursuing the children of God in these last days…Looking for the weak, the embattled and the weary ones,… These seducing spirits will effect **_doctrines, convictions and important life decisions_**, and like most predators, they look for **_easy prey_**. Sexual predators often target children,…The Apostle Paul admonishes the Saints: ***That we henceforth be no more children, tossed to and fro, and carried about with every wind of doctrine, by the sleight of men, and cunning craftiness, whereby they lie in wait to deceive;*** **Ephesians 4:14**

In these last days seducing spirits will gain access to the Body of Christ through False Teachers and False Doctrines Crafted by Satan himself to deceive mankind. Be on the lookout for my upcoming book, "Grace with a Conscience", that exposes this phenomenon. The responsibility of the believer is to remain submitted to God in every trial, and to resist and overcome the evil one! **NOTE:** There is a difference between one who is given to evil willfully, and one who has been seduced when in a weakened state. In many cases, there are precious Saints of God who simply "gave heed" to these seducers when they were in a weakened state, ...these need our help returning to the Lord. Judas was translated from the power of Darkness into the Kingdom of light, just like John or James, but after receiving this great light, he Fornicated with the Serpent, and ultimately surrendered this great light, turning back unto the darkness of night.

Take heed therefore that the light which is in thee be not darkness. **Luke 11:35**

Even if you've fallen, failed God in some way, or turned back to darkness, God has provided a way back!

*Let us draw near with a true heart in full assurance of faith, having our hearts **sprinkled** from an evil conscience, and our bodies washed with pure water.* **Hebrews 10:22**

A Sprinkle a day is the Kingdom way! Return to the Father in sincerity, and be secure in His unconditional Love for you, His love is greater than all!

3 steps to freedom from spiritual fornication

1.) If we are to avoid fornicating with the Serpent, we must refuse to entertain his lying voice. The Serpent, here, presents a clear lie to Eve, which she should have refused!

God said:

...thou shalt surely die **Genesis 2:17**

And the serpent said unto the woman,

Ye shall not surely die: **Genesis 3:4**

The Remedy: What should you do when God tells you something, and the Devil contradicts it? Call the Devil a Liar, cast down the imagination, step on his head and keep it moving!

2.) Look for the good in everything, God may show you another perspective...

And the LORD had respect unto Abel and to his offering: But unto Cain and to his offering he had not respect

Genesis 4:4-5

The Remedy: As we know, Cain went on to murder his brother Abel in an envious rage. This was Cain's opportunity to learn from his brother, but instead, he murdered his teacher. He had the wrong perspective of correction. Think before you act: Submit to God, resist the Devil. Humility comes before honor.

In example 1 &2 it is clear that entertaining the wrong voice can be a deadly undertaking

3.) Call on the name of the Lord, for in your weakness, his strength is made perfect...

For thou hast been a shelter for me, and a strong tower from the enemy. **Psalms 61:3**

The Remedy: If you sense that there is an enemy presence within your thought-life, call on the name of Jesus in resistance to it, and it will flee from you! That name breaks every stronghold . Remember to declare: I AM FULLY SUBMITTED TO GOD. And again Speak the name of Jesus. I have experienced instant freedom from extreme demonic attacks by Speaking out his name with boldness. In some cases, it is not necessary to say any other words, just **JESUS!**

attend to my words; *Proverbs 4:19-21*-note page

attend to my words; *Proverbs 4:19-21*-**note page**

Spiritual Immune Systems (The Preservers of Purpose)

Dominating Emotions, like many natural toxins and poisons, attack systemically to break down the body and soul by weakening the physical and spiritual immune systems. They are truly poisoners of purpose. It has been my observation that bitterness, in particular, behaves most like a virus seeking to attack and overload the immune system (Faith, Hope and Love). These (3) Three Powerful Kingdom Attributes act like the E.P.A. (Environmental Protection Agency), they establish the rule or law for what is hazardous or unsafe within our internal environments. These rules, however, are often broken and the consequences often untold. Bitterness can also mimic a sperm cell, swimming until it finds something to fertilize (the Heart and Soul). Jesus would have none of this, not even to help the pain. Not even to drown his sorrows.

It was here that Jesus again overcame (preserving the internal environment of heart, mind and soul), the man of sorrows (Isaiah 53:3), kept anchoring his soul to divine purpose... I believe that our Lord Jesus Christ glimpsed into the future and saw the billions of unredeemed souls for which he had come to die..., alas, Breakthrough to Joy!

...who for the Joy that was set before Him (which was you and I), He endured the Cross and despised the shame.

Hebrews 12:2

One observation I have made over the years is that God often preserves on the basis of purpose. This is a pattern for us to follow. It behooves us to protect our internal environments, and to build up our immune systems (Faith, Hope and Love). By doing this, we Preserve our Purpose! Remember the Words that God has spoken over your life, they reflect your continuing purpose. Anything that works against your purpose, is no friend of yours. It is an adversary, a hindrance, and it must be destroyed! Pray this prayer with me:

PRAYER:

Father I take dominion and authority over every destructive spiritual root operating within me. I ask you to unravel each destructive root from my soul and release me from every dominating emotion. I diffuse the power of such emotions to rule over me, and entrust my soul into your care, in Jesus name. Father, as I experience the freedom that comes from your Power and Love, help me to preserve and protect my purpose.

attend to my words; <u>Proverbs 4:19-21</u>**-note page**

Dominating Emotions
(Paying the Toll)

What is a Dominating Emotion? It is an emotional stronghold that is brought about or created as the direct result of satanic attacks, or a traumatic experience, that assumes a dominant position within the human personality. [One example might be of someone who's had lifelong struggles with rejection, a dominating emotion and spiritual root, that resulted from their parents divorcing during their early childhood.] These and other dominating emotions have taken their toll on our lives, demanding payment every time they pop up. Like a toll booth appearing randomly in the middle of the street, out of nowhere, bringing our lives to a screeching halt! Pay up now, or you cannot go any further! Often, the payment is unjust, and usually cruel. Sleeplessness, weight gain, depression, loneliness, alcoholism, sexual addictions, promiscuity, drug use, stresses, suicides and countless other struggles can be traced back to one or more dominating emotions. Yes, it is true, our spiritual battles, and traumatic life events often weigh the heaviest upon the frailty of our emotions. We will discuss six (6) Dominating Emotions, their causes, effects and biblical remedies at length in the coming chapters.

Behold, I give unto you power to tread on serpents and scorpions, and over all the power of the enemy: and nothing shall by any means hurt you. **Luke 10:19**

These Serpents and Scorpions represent demonic methods of attack...the serpent mounts a **frontal attack** using it's head and fangs to bite, while the Scorpion uses a **rear stinger**, and can attack while appearing to retreat. This says to me that we must be as diligent about our spiritual and emotional health when we "feel good", as we are when we are in a battle. Even when the scorpion retreats, he can be dangerous. Jesus promised his disciples power (authority) over all the power (ability) of the enemy, and freedom from hurt! But sometimes it feels like the enemy is treading us down in our emotions, and weighing us down in our minds. Some have questioned, "Is this promise for us today"? "Can we be free from mental and emotional assault". The answer is a resounding YES! But there are some steps to take. This power (authority) that Jesus has given us is most certainly to be appropriated for use against warfare in the mind and emotions. This is the frontline battlefield for most believers today....A Kingdom Fortified Mind is the Devil's worst nightmare.

Wherefore gird up the loins of your mind, be sober, and **hope to the end** *for the grace that is to be brought unto you at the revelation of Jesus Christ;* **1Peter 1:13**

The Framework for most every Miracle is Hope... Kingdom Hope effects perspective

Our ability to have hope in any situation is directly effected by our perspective. Many things effect our perspective, but nothing more powerfully than the Word of God. The Fortified Kingdom Mind is a mind that has become a storehouse for The Word of God, and a Treasury of Kingdom Truths, [scarcely is there a victorious believer where there is little or no Kingdom Truth INVESTMENT / RE-INVESTMENT].

<u>DECLARE THIS WITH ME:</u> "I HAVE A FORTIFIED KINGDOM MIND", and make this your DAILY CONFESSION! And then, go and FORTIFY it with the WORD of GOD! EXALT God's Word as FINAL AUTHORITY, and it WILL sober your thoughts and emotions! This is a very important part of our emotional and spiritual health. Caution, Stay away from HOPE STEALERS! Jesus is coming to set you free!

We will be discussing the above scripture 1 Peter 1:13 at length in the coming chapters!

attend to my words; incline thine ear unto my sayings. <u>Proverbs 4:19-21</u>-**note page**

attend to my words; incline thine ear unto my sayings. <u>Proverbs 4:19-21</u>**-note page**

A Vesture Dipped in Blood

The Revelation of Jesus Christ spoken of by Peter (1 Peter 1:13) is the spontaneous, joy-giving, advantage assuring, life carrying truth that neutralizes the power of every unfounded lie, every twisted tale and treacherous attack. This continuous Revelation can come through a download from Heaven, a voice from Heaven, an upload from the Holy Spirit, a dream, a vision, etc... **The Revelation of Jesus Christ** can also come through a Personal Visitation from the Lord .

2:00 am- Revelation/Visitation from the Lord...

After a freak accident, (my head vs. the edge of my car door) guess who won? I began experiencing significant head pain and booming sounds due to a not so mild concussion. I had forgotten that I had this freak accident because it jarred my memory. As the symptoms persisted for weeks, the enemy attempted to invade my mind-space with thoughts of doom all day long. I endured a barrage of thought-possibilities (lies and satanic innuendos) about the source of my head pain and the other bizarre symptoms I was having. I laid down at around 10:00 pm to rest and hear from God, only to be awakened by a severe demonic attack from two demonic spiritual beings...One was Fear and the other was Torment. [I was familiar with these spirits as they had once held me captive and produced a Dominating Emotion of Fear within my life] I was awakened by what felt like a blow to my head, it was as if I was fighting two men, but I was in a Spiritual battle and their weapons were Fear and Terror. We will discuss fear and the remedy in a coming chapter. As I sat up startled in my bed, immediately the Lord Jesus arrived and Spoke Boldly in an audible voice saying "a Vesture Dipped in Blood", and then He repeated it again "a Vesture Dipped in Blood"...I immediately understood that he wanted me to use this as a weapon; that he was revealing a mystery, that I knew nothing about; that would protect me from injury; that nothing would by any means hurt me. I then began to declare "a Vesture Dipped in Blood", "A Vesture Dipped in Blood"...As I declared these words, the battle was turned in my favor, the relentless demonic attack broke, and I was able to sleep the rest of the night in peaceful rest. Later that morning I found that scripture in the book of Revelation.

*And I saw heaven opened, and behold a white horse; and he that sat upon him was called Faithful and True, and in righteousness **he doth judge and make war**. * His eyes were as a flame of fire, and on his head were many crowns; and he had a name written, that no man knew, but he himself. * **And he was clothed with a vesture dipped in blood:** and his name is called The Word of God. *And the armies which were in heaven followed him upon white horses, clothed in fine linen, white and clean. *And out of his mouth goeth a sharp sword, that with it he should smite the nations: and he shall rule them with a rod of* *iron: and he treadeth the winepress of the fierceness and wrath of Almighty God. *And he hath on his vesture and on his thigh a name written, KING OF KINGS, AND LORD OF LORDS.*

Rev 19:11-16

IT IS CLEAR THROUGH SCRIPTURE THAT THIS VESTURE DIPPED IN BLOOD IS HIS WAR GARMENT! JESUS IS THE WARRIOR KING OF GLORY! JESUS WAS REVEALED IN MY BATTLE! JESUS WANTS TO BE REVEALED IN YOUR BATTLE TO DEFEAT DEMONIC SPIRITS AND DOMINATING EMOTIONS!

DECLARE THIS WITH ME:
"I AM CLOTHED IN A VESTURE DIPPED IN BLOOD"

I am learning to consistently "Gird up the loins of my mind" and "hope to the end for the grace which is to come unto me at the REVELATION OF JESUS CHRIST"! It is through the Girding up of our minds, binding them to and with the Word of God that we become spiritually sober and become recipients of endless hope. This hope manifests as courage to stand and see the Salvation of the Lord! As one who has endured several attacks against the mind and emotions, I have discovered that the enemy sends darts at random towards our lives. He then observes our responses and looks for any weakness that he can exploit. If he finds a particular area of vulnerability, he is relentless in his attack, and consistent in his efforts to defeat, discourage and destroy. If the enemy is able to gain a place of control within the human soul, whether by demonic entrance or mental snares (Imaginations that have lodged within the mind and refuse to let go) DOMINATING EMOTIONS WILL RESULT.

Peter is telling us to have our minds readied (Girded), prepared and equipped for an enemy strike or invasion attempt at any time [these can come through thoughts, imaginations, torments, delusions, magnifications of "what if's", imbalances of rationale, traumas from encounters with people etc.]. Peter also teaches that sobriety is a necessity in the battlefield of the mind. It is then and only then that we can "hope to the end for the grace" that will be brought unto us "at the Revelation of Jesus Christ". The Grace that I received during the previously mentioned attack was this Revelation of and from Jesus Christ!

"A Vesture Dipped in Blood"

I constantly declare this over myself and others as defense against spiritual attacks and dominating emotions!

I suggest that you do the same as a believer and follower of Christ. This was revealed to me as a weapon of defense by the Lord himself!

attend to my words; Proverbs 4:19-21-note page

attend to my words; <u>Proverbs 4:19-21</u>*-note page*

The Procreative Mind

Wherefore gird up the loins of your mind, be sober, and hope to the end for the grace that is to be brought unto you at the revelation of Jesus Christ; As obedient children, not fashioning yourselves according to the former lusts in your ignorance:

1 Peter 1:13-14 (KJV)

We are back here observing this scripture again in 1 Peter chapter 1. The word for "loins" in the Greek is ***ozphuz*** (os-foos) which means (*procreative power*). The "loins" of the physical body are given to us for the purpose of reproduction/procreation. The mind also has the power to create or generate powerful realities. The health of the human soul depends on a strong defense, and offense at the gate of the mind to protect the will and emotions from ungodly influences. The words "be sober" reveal a very necessary truth. When under spiritual, mental, physical or emotional attack, the first responses are the most important ones. Trained soldiers are not flustered by enemy fire because they are readied and prepared for battle at all times. They have "a readied mind". They are sober. This is an offensive, as well as a defensive mindset. Readiness, not just to defend, but to strike a blow at the enemy by declaring the truth in faith... Peter admonishes us to *"hope to the end for the grace that is to be brought unto you"*

1 Peter 1:13

In other words, Peter is telling us that there is endless hope available, real hope. Not wishful thinking or positive thinking, but a KING! KEEP YOUR MIND STAYED ON JESUS!

This Hope enables the Procreative (Reality Producing) Power of the Mind to Picture or See the Promises of God for freedom in every situation. Grace delivers this new hope, and a Fresh revealing of the Son of God to our Hearts… Jesus, Exalted, Roaring like a Lion! When we envision our Savior, our Champion, our Healer as He is…We will return To and With Joy! Our clearest views and greatest realities must be of the Kingdom of God. The days are over for half-hearted faith and barely believing believers. We must invest in the eternal, this life is but a vapor! Real Hope comes from a Real God, a Real Christ, and a Real Kingdom with Real Power!

God has never lost a battle, He can't lose, and neither can we! Lift up a prayer to God like Daniel in the Lions Den. Lift up a prayer to God like Moses at the edge of the Red Sea. Lift up a prayer to God like Paul and Silas in that Philippian jail. Lift up a prayer to God like Esther did before she went in to see the King! You are about to receive your oil, your healing, your miracle, your comfort, your answer, your intervention, your Father has been working it out behind the scenes, and your hour of visitation is right here! Be sober, be ready…"hope to the end".

Even if you do not yet have the spiritual/mental training

or discipline necessary to stand firmly when afflicted or distressed, begin to assert the anointing of the Holy Spirit through prayer, we that are Christ's are ALL Anointed! The Holy Spirit will ignite prayers that avail much, and even if you are not able to pray, He is making intercession for you with groaning which cannot be uttered. (Romans 8:26)

Fear, worry, anger etc., as Dominating Emotions, have tried us all, but they are no match for the Spirit of God. By choosing to pray and by girding up the loins (closing the gates) of our minds, we are heightening our walls of defense and strengthening our shields of faith. As we speak, we grasp the Sword of the Spirit, which is the Word of God, and berate every mental intruder with a two-edged sword. **Remember to Speak: Rev 19:13**

"A VESTURE DIPPED IN BLOOD"! Spoken out by Jesus, and to be repeated by you and I. I believe this to be a mystery of the Kingdom.

A NOTE OF CAUTION: PETER WRITES:

As obedient children, not fashioning yourselves according to the former lusts in your ignorance:

1 Peter 1:13-14 (KJV)

Obedience and abstinence from fleshly lusts help keep our mental and physical loins gird up. Dominating emotions are not always easy to subdue, and the evil spirits that seduce and entrap are not always easy to drive out. Once freedom is realized, it is imperative that we keep iniquity at bay, and give demon spirits no place to re-afflict our souls. They are infamous for seducing us back into bondage, and then condemning us for our downfalls.

Enlist the Family of GOD

Lest Satan should get an advantage of us: for we are not ignorant of his devices. **2 Corinthians 2:11**

Notice here that Paul says "us"…When a brother or Sister in Christ is under attack, "we" are all called to action...Whether to Protect, Intercede, or to Stand in the way … We are our brothers keeper! The enemy of our souls devises specific strategies when targeting a Child of God….He studies our behavioral responses to each attack to determine our areas of weakness…When he finds a weakness, he will exploit it again and again until it is fortified by the Kingdom of God. Partnering in prayer and intercession with other believers keeps a partial covering over you at all times. It is important that we enlist the prayers of other Saints during every spiritual and emotional battle. Lest Satan should get an advantage of us!

DECLARE THIS WITH ME:
I AM NOT ALONE IN THIS BATTLE. THE HOLY SPIRIT AND MY SPIRITUAL PARTNERS ARE PRAYING FOR ME [FIND A PRAYER PARTNER YOU CAN TRUST]

Once again, Fear, Shame, Rejection etc., are all enemies of hope, but they are no match for The Procreative Mind, Girded by Visions and Revelations from Christ, Fortified by God's Word, Strengthened through God's Grace, and Covered by Christ's Blood. I pray that the Light of Revelation received through this book is already defeating Dominating Emotions, and releasing Kingdom Freedom into your life. Let's looks at some practical steps.

STEP 1. GIRD UP THE LOINS:

In other words, by binding our minds to Kingdom Truths, we shut the doors of access within our minds to Satan's lies. It is not just the truth, but the anointing of truth that sets us free! READING-WRITING-PRAYING what has been revealed, or brought unto you at the Revelation of Jesus Christ will ensure a READIED MIND!...Remember, I Declared...Rev 19:13 "A VESTURE DIPPED IN BLOOD"!

STEP 2. RECORD THE MYSTERY:

Always remember to write down the promise, vision, word, or message received. This Vision, Word etc. that is brought unto you is a MYSTERY of the KINGDOM of HEAVEN... MYSTERIES ARE NOT DEFENSIBLE BY THE ENEMY...He has no advantage or method of defense, because Mystery Truths are hidden from him...All he can use is the same old fear tactics...but When a

Kingdom Mystery has been revealed...Satan is at a great, great disadvantage... If you got hit with an unexpected punch, remember Jesus is in your corner...and even in the 12th round he has a strategy for Victory...The King is Coming!

STEP 3. GIVE HIM THE PRAISE:

Just about the hardest thing to do when facing a Spiritual Attack or Dominating Emotion is to PRAISE GOD. I know, it doesn't make any sense, right? Well actually, Praise causes us to focus on the abilities, attributes and all around goodness of our God. Praise brings God on the scene, into full view, ...Glory!

attend to my words; <u>Proverbs 4:19-21</u>*-note page*

attend to my words; *Proverbs 4:19-21*-**note page**

Prepared For Battle
(By the Spirit of Truth)

Pearl Harbor was a classic example of the dangers of unreadiness. The surprise Japanese attack against U.S. Forces at Pearl Harbor leveled American military resources in that area and cost multiple lives in the process. Pearl Harbor was a well planned surprise attack that caught U.S. Military Forces sleeping.

Though the Battle rages on, **The Holy Spirit** who is all knowing, never sleeps, and will always reveal the attack plans of the enemy to God's children (It helps us to hear if we are listening to and spending time with God). We will not have victory without Him. The early Apostles and Prophets depended upon the Holy Spirit for guidance, direction, judgment, wisdom, utterance, power, fortitude, giftings, and perhaps above all, the ability to remain sober in the most trying times through the fruit of the Spirit. He enables us to remain free under fire! He prays for us! And when he gives the command, we need to make a preemptive strike. In Battle, the First Strike can determine the difference between victory and defeat, but even if the enemy got in the first strike, God has an Atom Bomb for the Devil! Prophetic believer's can also be of great help in disclosing the plans or devices of the enemy, *before* they come to pass. The key is preparation and readiness. This is a part of remaining *sober*. 1 Peter 1:13

attend to my words; *Proverbs 4:19-21*-*note page*

Towers of Unbelief (must fall down)

*For though we walk in the flesh, we do not war after the flesh: (For the weapons of our warfare are not carnal, but mighty through God to the pulling down of strong holds;) Casting down **imaginations**, and every high thing that exalteth itself against the knowledge of God, and bringing into captivity every thought to the obedience of Christ;*

2 Cor 10:3-5

This passage of scripture clearly exposes the strategy of the enemy. If he can captivate the mind, he has won one of the strongest gates of human existence. Countless believers and unbelievers alike struggle with a barrage of ***imagination*** thoughts on a daily basis that are contrary to the will of God, and exalt themselves against the knowledge of God. I believe these Imaginations to be spiritual assignments against the mind, because they are connected in the previous scripture to "high things". These "things" are strongholds in the mind that can become like towers that obstruct our view of the Kingdom. They are produced by Imaginations that are allowed to build "high things" within us without resistance. These Imaginations can work against the mind while we are awake or while we are asleep. When we are awake they will often manifest as intrusive thoughts that "exalt themselves against the knowledge of God". When we are asleep, they may subconsciously afflict our minds and effect our waking moments with fear and sorrow. *If you awake with fear, most often there has been some sort of Satanic oppression around you while you slept, and/or a dominating emotion that has become inflamed.*

Prayer for Protection (While Sleeping): *Satan I forbid you to infiltrate my <u>dream life</u>, <u>thought life</u>, or <u>subconscious life</u> in the name of the Lord Jesus Christ by the Power of the Holy Spirit. Pray this nightly, and it will erect a gate over your mind while you sleep! It has been very effective for me, and many that I have had the privilege to pray for.*

Every time we cast down an Imagination we prevent or deter the erection of a **Tower "high thing"**. If on the other hand, we entertain an Imagination. we invite a **Tower "high thing"** to be erected in the mind, that will eventually obstruct our view of the Kingdom of God.

When the children of Israel were preparing to enter the promise land, their were some that had **"towers of unbelief"**, "high things" established within their minds so that they **could not believe the promises of God**. When the "ten spies" went in to spy out the land, "eight" of them returned with an evil report. These "high things" gave place to a spirit of fear in their hearts that would infect the majority of the people. ...Likewise when God was giving them Jericho, it was necessary to flatten the walls

(Towers)...

> *But Joshua had commanded the people, "Do not give a war cry, do not raise your voices, do not say a word until the day I tell you to shout. Then shout!" ... So on the second day they marched around the city once and returned to the camp. They did this for six days. On the seventh day, they got up at daybreak and marched around the city seven times in the same manner, except that on that day they circled the city seven times. The seventh time around, when the priests sounded the trumpet blast, Joshua commanded the people, "Shout! For the LORD has given you the city!...when the people gave a loud shout, the wall collapsed; so every man charged straight in, and they took the city.*
>
> **Joshua 6:10-16,20**

Towers of Unbelief are usually built over a long period of time, and can reach up very high...like the "walls of Jericho", these need to come down before we can take back the city (the mind). The instruction that Joshua gave the people was to **"Shout, for the Lord has given you the city"**. The literal walls of Jericho fell down through the power of a shout! The Shout, would have been powerless, though, if they had disobeyed the commandment of Joshua, to 1.) **"do not give a war cry"** 2.) **"do not raise your voices"** 3.) **"do not say a word until the day I tell you to shout"**. These commands from Joshua were the **"grace brought unto them at the revelation of Jesus Christ" 1 Peter 1:13,**...it was the indefensible Mystery of the Kingdom of

God with men. Their obedience to the instruction of Joshua would be the key to victory. Obedience to the *revealed* will, wisdom, command and instruction of the Lord is a simple but powerful key to victory in every situation. **Obedience brings God on the scene!**

Again, "High things" are to be avoided at all costs, lest we believe or embrace an evil report... When the "ten spies" went in to spy out the land, "eight" of them returned with an evil report. The "high things" in the mind, gave place to a spirit of fear in their hearts that, again, would infect the majority of the people. (See Chapter on *fear*)

Again, Imaginations must be cast down immediately before they can become "high things". One strategy that I have found to be very effective is to simply say **"NO IMAGINATIONS"**. By doing this, we are "girding up" the loins of our minds!

Imaginations and Familiar Spirits

Many years ago when I was a single young Christian, I rented rooms to three guys in my seven room apartment. One of them was new to Christ, and was battling with a drug problem. I knew that God had divinely connected us for that season to help him in his struggle. One morning when he went down to the basement to wash his clothes, he came across a painting that was so realistic it gave him an eerie feeling. As he continued to look at it, the eyes of the six or seven faces in the painting seemed to come to life and then a demon spoke to him and said "Don't tell Richard were down here".

The man came upstairs very afraid, and told me what had happened, refusing to go back into the basement after hearing this. He had encountering imaginations (demonic assignments against his mind) and a familiar spirit (demon) that spoke to him audibly. My first response was disbelief and slight fear, then, I "girt up the loins of my mind" and gathered my spiritual bearings, put on the whole armor of God, and proceeded to go down into the basement (alone). When I found the painting, it was as he described, and an unusual sense of evil, living evil, emanated from the eyes on the faces. This painting was attracting demon spirits of fear and witchcraft which knew my authority in Jesus Christ. Under the unction of the Holy Spirit, I prayed and broke the power of it's evil manifestation, and broke the painting into pieces, discarding it outside of the house. It was the fear (reverential, worshipful fear) of the Lord, that gave me victory over the Spirit of fear!

Authority over Demons with Long-Term Dominion

Those demons were intent on remaining in the basement of that apartment building (which I managed), and they had hoped to intimidate and paralyze my roommate by commanding him not to tell of their whereabouts. By doing this, they would have been able to maintain their territorial influence within the building and neighborhood. Thanks be to God, their position was exposed and their stronghold was destroyed. There are times when inanimate objects serve as shrines for evil manifestations. The objects themselves are not possessed, but they are offered or inviting to evil spirits because of their use, intention, influence or imagery.

The demons that possessed the man from Gerasenes cried out asking Jesus if He had come to torment them before their time... (Mark 5:1-20) They were willing though to relocate, rather than face the power and judgment of Jesus! I suggest a good read of the above mentioned verses to instill hope for your situation. This man was under complete spiritual and emotional domination, and yet, just one word from Jesus set him free!

Resisting Imagination Strategies

During a one hour period at my mobile food business/ministry I recognized an eerie pattern developing....one by one customer after customer told of relatives who had their limbs amputated because of underlying physical conditions. This would not have been unusual for maybe one or two in a week to share such a thing,...but four different people in one hour?....By the third person I just began to laugh as it became evident that there was a strategy in motion...a strategy to produce a stronghold of fear within my heart and a Dominating Emotion within my soul..

The enemy seeks to make the believer dysfunctional and unable to resist him by attaining a stronghold within his heart or soul to rule from.

On another occasion two friend's had a daughter who was under a spell of witchcraft cast on her by their angry "root working" landlord, who lived directly over them (by the way, she was a faithful member of a local church, who resorted to witchcraft when deemed necessary). Her all night chanting and "chicken feet" curses put their young child into a mind altering frenzy (causing her to shake and tremble in a confused and terrorized state) and filled the house with fear. All of their prayers seemed useless against the spell…It was at this point that I received a call from them, and proceeded to break the curse, discard the "chicken feet" and the spell was immediately broken over the child. The Power of Jesus name battled back demons of fear, captivity and witchcraft curses. **<u>A NOTE ON LAWLESSNESS:</u>** These friends had the same access that I had to the name of Jesus being believer's themselves, but at that time they were unmarried and their ongoing sinful relationship undoubtedly effected the way those demons perceived their authority/legal right to use the name of Jesus. i.e. *…and the evil spirit answered, and said, Jesus I know, Paul I know, but who are you?* **Acts 19:13-16**

God was gracious to them on that evening, and set their child free from demonic oppression. While willful and continual lawlessness is not the only reason for a lack of success in breaking witchcraft curses, IT IS ONE OF THE FIRST AREAS THAT THE ENEMY TARGETS TO RESIST EVICTION. Sobriety in mind, heart and body are very important. Ask the Lord for strength in your weaknesses. Ask for his mercy and the covering of his blood. Make some resolutions to be more obedient to God. And if at all possible, close every door of willful disobedience...Remember: Gird up the loins of your mind, be sober...the Grace is coming!

attend to my words; *Proverbs 4:19-21*-**note page**

attend to my words; incline thine ear unto my sayings. *Proverbs 4:19-21*-**note page**

Refraining The Mouth

After this opened Job his mouth, and cursed his day. **Job 3:1**

The devil could not kill Job because God forbid him to, so instead, he imposed great physical and emotional affliction upon Job's body, mind and soul and caused Job to hate his own life. This was the result of the many afflictions and attacks Job endured without knowledge of the spiritual warfare that was against him.

Therefore I will not refrain my mouth; I will speak in the anguish of my spirit; **<u>I will complain in the bitterness of my soul</u>**. *Am I a sea, or a whale, that thou settest a watch over me? When I say, My bed shall comfort me, my couch shall ease my complaint;* **Then thou scarest me with dreams, and terrifiest me through visions: So that my soul chooseth strangling, and death rather than my life. <u>I loathe it; I would not live alway: let me alone; for my days are vanity</u>**. **Job 7:11-16**

Job was ignorant of "Satan's devices". These night terror's were not the work of the Lord, but the works of the Devil. These attacks were highly successful against Job's soul, turning Job against himself through self-loathing and self-rejection..

Lest Satan should get an advantage of us: for we are not ignorant of his devices. **2 Cor 2:11**

Maybe you've been there, pain filled, under severe attack, cursing your day. Rest assured beloved, Jesus is assured REST! He takes no delight in tormenting his people. Gird up the loins of your mind, be sober and hope to the end for the grace that is to be brought unto you at **The Revelation of Jesus Christ**! God has a Word for you that is going to turn the tables on the enemy. Speak His Word Only!

It is very important that we not succumb to the enemy's strategy, and begin to speak death into our situations. Thank God for His providential mercy that prevented Job's hopeless words from coming to pass. Job would see better days, blessed days, full recovery and increase, but in his darkest moments...he cursed his day.

NEVER CURSE YOUR DAY, YOU ARE FEARFULLY AND WONDERFULLY MADE!

The Holy Spirit provides the advantage in warfare through the prophetic anointing (See Joel 2:28) . Believer's today need not succumb to this kind of satanic onslaught with feelings of hopelessness, confusion and suicidal words. Job went through a process of justification, but Jesus has already declared us RIGHTEOUS, and Jesus himself is both Lawyer and Evidential Proof of our Righteousness. The Verdict is already in, and He was sentenced in our place, that we might be called the Righteousness of God in Him! When the accuser of the brethren comes before God in these times to challenge God's testimony of Righteousness over us, he must deal with our Advocate (lawyer) with the Father...Jesus Christ the Righteous! Jesus is the both the Advocate and the evidence!

Proof positive of your legal right to victory

Exhibit a.) The Blood [Shed for the remission of sins, and continuous power over the adversary] *And they overcame him by the blood of the Lamb, and the word of their testimony...*
Revelation 12:11

Exhibit b.) His Hands & Feet [Completed the Works of God and were pierced] *Behold my hands and my feet, that it is I myself: handle me, and see;* **Luke 24:39**

Exhibit c.) His Side and His Head [Wounded for our transgression and the overcoming of mental and emotional warfare (Dominating Emotions)] *Behold, he cometh with clouds; and every eye shall see him, and they also which pierced him:*
Revelation 1:7

Exhibit d.) His Back [His Stripes bought our Right to Total Healing] Case Dismissed! *by whose stripes ye were healed.*
1 Peter 2:24
Matt 8:16-17

attend to my words; incline thine ear unto my sayings. <u>Proverbs 4:19-21</u>-**note page**

attend to my words; incline thine ear unto my sayings. <u>Proverbs 4:19-21</u>-**note page**

Jesus was our Job

The Book of Job (Snapshot)

God was establishing Job's righteousness through a test of affliction. He declared Job to be a <u>morally perfect man</u>, but not a <u>sinless man</u>. Satan declared that Job's moral integrity was due to God's blessing and favor, but that it would not hold up under other circumstances (Satanic Attack). It would all hinge on this one statement "he will curse you to his face" (Job never did this, but ***he wrongfully cursed himself***). Even Job's wife encouraged him [under satanic influence] to curse God and die.

But he said unto her, Thou speakest as one of the foolish women speaketh. What? shall we receive good at the hand of God, and shall we not receive evil? <u>In all this did not Job sin with his lips.</u> **Job 2:10**

Here it is clear that the sin referred to was that of "Cursing God". But Job would have done better not to have cursed himself either. This Job did because of his great despair, and God Himself felt the pain of Job's affliction.

And the LORD said unto Satan, Hast thou considered my servant Job, that there is none like him in the earth, a perfect and an upright man, one that feareth God, and escheweth evil? and still he holdeth fast his integrity, although thou movedst me against him, to destroy him without cause. **Job 2:3**

Throughout his lengthy trial, Job asks this question in many ways;...How can man be just with God? If there was one overwhelming purpose for , or message from Job's trial, it was **the message of JUSTIFICATION!**

I know it is so of a truth: but how should man be just with God?
Job 9:2 KJV

If I justify myself, mine own mouth shall condemn me: if I say, I am perfect, it shall also prove me perverse.
Job 9:20 KJV

Behold now, I have ordered my cause; I know that I shall be justified.
Job 13:18 KJV

O that one might plead for a man with God, as a man pleadeth for his neighbour!
Job 16:21 KJV

Job longs for an advocate with God to plead his case, We have one to plead ours!

My little children, these things write I unto you, that ye sin not. And if any man sin, we have an advocate with the Father, Jesus Christ the righteous:
1John 2:1 KJV

For I know that my redeemer liveth, and that he shall stand at the latter day upon the earth:
Job 19:25 KJV

Whether you've passed the test like Job, or miserably failed in your trial of affliction, or have fallen victim to a dominating emotion, or maybe even been bitter with God Himself,...know that Jesus has come to bring justification and peace with God to all who believe and call upon His name. Like The Apostle Paul, who got bitten by a Viper (in Acts Chapter 28) and was protected from it's venom...You can shake that serpent off of you, and into the fire, and lay hold of the previously mentioned benefits of Christ's wounds. [see Refraining the Mouth]

attend to my words; <u>Proverbs 4:19-21</u>**-note page**

attend to my words; <u>Proverbs 4:19-21</u>*-note page*

Bitterness Part 1

Bitterness is a root that causes great blindness in the human heart. It has a way of souring all that is good in the eyes of it's victims.

I once had an opportunity to counsel a couple that had gone through some challenges in their marriage. One of the partners was bent on reconciliation and focused on recovery, and while the other partner seemed to be advancing in spiritual growth and maturity, there remained an underlying root of bitterness that laid dormant waiting for the right heart condition to spring up from. After months of forward progress in the marriage, a jarring emotional event exposed this root, and it sprang up like a wildfire and ravaged the new found fruit in their marriage. This root of Bitterness lashed out at the other partner by digging up old wounds which produced new pain, increased deceptions and accusations while exacting torments in the process. This root of bitterness had become a tool of the enemy through the power of words. The accused partner was able to stand though, by recognizing that a root of bitterness had left a doorway open for this new level of spiritual warfare in the marriage.

Wherefore take unto you the whole armour of God, that ye may be able to withstand in the evil day, and having done all, to stand. **Ephesians 6:13 (KJV)**

Bitterness is Satan's Brew and a great inhibitor of healing

*Wherefore lift up the hands which hang down, and the feeble knees; And make straight paths for your feet, lest that which is lame be turned out of the way; but let it rather be healed. Follow peace with all men, and holiness, without which no man shall see the Lord: Looking diligently lest any man fail of the grace of God; lest any **root of bitterness springing up trouble you**, and thereby many be defiled.* **Hebrews 12:12-15 (KJV)**

...a little unforgiveness (which hinders healing), a little resentment and even a dash of loathing hatred will fuel thoughts of retaliation, revenge and fleshly indulgence. These sentiments are surely a product of the works of the flesh (Gal 5:19-20) and demonic oppressions (Acts 10:38).

Satan undoubtedly stood brooding after his ejection from Heaven. He cannot forget, because he will not forgive God's judgment against his own rebellion. The devil still holds bitterness against God in his heart for casting him out of heaven like lightning. A judgment displayed before all of the angels of God, and before the fallen angels who followed him in his defeat. Satan approached mankind in the form of a serpent, a hissing, fork tongued creature with bad intentions. Bitterness is the venom of the serpent. **Note:** Bitterness is at the root of many of today's physical diseases.

A "Hiss" is defined as a sound expressing disapproval or dislike… It is the sound of bitterness.

It has been said that some people will not forgive you for the things that they have done <u>to you</u>.

… But if ye have bitter envying and strife in your hearts, glory not, and lie not against the truth. This wisdom descendeth not from above, but is earthly, sensual, devilish

James 3:13-15

Bitterness is here called devilish wisdom. When Satan was in heaven he became filled with presumptuous pride, but when he fell (was cast down) from Heaven he became embittered and hissed at God's creation. This bitterness was first evidenced in the heart of Cain.

And Adam knew Eve his wife; and she conceived, and bare Cain, and said, I have gotten a man from the L<small>ORD</small>. And she again bare his brother Abel. And Abel was a keeper of sheep, but Cain was a tiller of the ground. And in process of time it came to pass, that Cain brought of the fruit of the ground an offering unto the L<small>ORD</small>. And Abel, he also brought of the firstlings of his flock and of the fat thereof. And the L<small>ORD</small> had respect unto Abel and to his offering: But unto Cain and to his offering he had not respect. ***And Cain was <u>very wroth</u>, and his countenance fell.***

Genesis 4:1-5

We see here that Cain was very angry because God favored his brother's offering over his own. This would have been a good opportunity for Cain to learn from his brother Abel. Instead, though, he allowed a root of bitterness to form and grow in his heart, and he killed his teacher.

And the LORD said unto Cain, Why art thou wroth? and why is thy countenance fallen? If thou doest well, shalt thou not be accepted? and if thou doest not well, **sin lieth at the door**. *And unto thee shall be his desire, and thou shalt rule over him.*

Genesis 4:6-8

Cain was undoubtedly fornicating with the serpent here, and his offering was reflective of this influence of evil. A NOTE ON THIS: " Never let the devil influence your offering"! After this, the serpent imparted bitterness and jealousy...

Cain didn't take authority over the sin that was lying at the door of his heart as God had directed him, instead, he invited the sin of bitter resentment into his heart which gave the devil a vice-like grip within him. The bible calls this a stronghold. Once the stronghold was secured, he invaded this heart territory and sent in a strongman called "murder" to rule in his heart. It wasn't very long before Cain lashed out at Abel, his brother, in a murderous rage.

It is so very important that we guard our hearts against every corrupt seed. A root cannot develop unless a seed is first sown. The Holy Spirit is a wonderful helper in the area of instant repentance. He will bring conviction to the Christian when his dominion (the heart of man) has been tainted by a foreign substance. The Holy Spirit is a friend, a helper, an advocate and intercessor for the believer. He convicts us of sin. He gets grieved when we allow unholy things to come into his house. The vast majority of Old Testament believers saw God's displeasure through outward signs and acts of correction or displays of anger. But, the New Testament believer being under grace must not take God's grace for granted. We must understand the "Laws of Grace" given through the foundational wisdom of the Apostles and Prophets, Jesus Christ being our Chief Teacher, Lord and the Cornerstone of the Faith. Jesus taught us about the precious nature of the Holy Spirit, and how the Father esteems him.

Verily I say unto you, All sins shall be forgiven unto the sons of men, and blasphemies wherewith soever they shall blaspheme: But he that shall blaspheme against the Holy Ghost hath never forgiveness, but is in danger of eternal damnation: Because they said, He hath an unclean spirit. **Mark 3:28-30**

What mankind spoke against Jesus will be forgiven, but it is not so with the Holy Spirit. The Holy Spirit is the Untouchable aspect of the Godhead. He is the Very Nature of the Father. God has chosen to indwell every believer, with and by the Holy Spirit, thus we need to listen to his direction and be keen to his displeasure. When he is grieved, we should feel it. When he's been quenched, we should know it. When he is stirring we should yield. When he is moving, we should allow it. When he is unctioning, we should speak it. When he is anointing, we should acknowledge it. When he is speaking, we should hear it. When he is separating persons for public service, we should affirm it. When he is teaching, we should receive it. When he is leading and guiding, we should follow him. When he is warning us, we should take heed. There are not enough pages to describe the benefits of knowing the Holy Spirit, but of this we can be sure. We need him.

The Apostle Paul confirms our duty as Christians concerning the Holy Spirit.

...Quench not the Spirit. **1 Thess 5:19**

Let no corrupt communication proceed out of your mouth, but that which is good to the use of edifying, that it may minister grace unto the hearers. And **grieve not the holy Spirit of God**, *whereby ye are sealed unto the day of redemption.* **Let all bitterness**, *and wrath, and anger, and clamour, and evil speaking, be put away from you, with all malice: And be ye kind one to another, tenderhearted,* ***forgiving one another****, even as God for Christ's sake hath forgiven you.* **Eph 4:29-32**

After all, we are "the temple of the Holy Ghost". It is at the time of sowing that we have the greatest defense against a stronghold. Even if a seed gets planted in our hearts, like anger or bitterness or resentment, it can be dug out easily through a conscious rejection once it is discovered. But, if when we recognize the ungodly seed, we entertain or embrace it in order to satisfy our flesh, we are at risk for the formation of a root, which if left to grow will surely become a stronghold.

What say I then? that the idol is any thing, or that which is offered in sacrifice to idols is any thing? But I say, that the things which the Gentiles sacrifice, they sacrifice to devils, and not to God: and I would not that ye should have fellowship with devils. Ye cannot drink the cup of the Lord, and the cup of devils...

1 Cor 10:20-22

The Apostle Paul here is warning the Corinthian Church to abstain from eating things, foods, etc. that were sacrificed to idols. He noted that the sacrifices and the idols were meaningless in themselves, but that the demons behind such practices were real. He went on to teach that we should not drink from the cup of the Lord, and the cup of devils. The moral of this teaching is this: be careful what you take into your body and into your spirit,...especially when you know what's in the cup!

When the devil tries to pour you a cup of bitterness, refuse to drink it in! I have heard many people say "I have a right to be bitter" , because of some truly terrible event that has happened to them. But, bitterness is not a right at all, but a bait from Satan into further destruction of the soul, giving him greater power to inflict wounds.

We will do much better if we choose to drink the cup of

blessing. We are to bless our human enemies, and not curse them. And, though our anger may be justified, justified anger does not justify sin. In addition to this, the enemy is always trying to seduce us to take off our armor and get us to operate outside of the "laws of grace" in order to gain an advantage over us in some other area in our lives.

Be ye angry, and sin not: let not the sun go down upon your wrath: Neither give place to the devil.
Eph 4:26-27

This is not to be confused with being passive in opposition to our spiritual enemy and adversary, the devil, whom we are to *"resist steadfast in the faith"*.

Be sober, be vigilant; because your adversary the devil, as a roaring lion, walketh about, seeking whom he may devour: Whom resist stedfast in the faith.
1 Peter 5:8-9

Perhaps the greatest area of warfare in the believer's life is in the area of the inner life. We may feel like we are alone at times, and that God does not see the battle. It may seem like we are resisting the devil at every turn...But the Holy Spirit desires to coach us, and give us winning strategies against the wiles of the devil. To teach us how to rule our own spirit, and govern our own souls as we yield to his Holy nature, and die to our old natures.

The Spirit of wisdom and revelation is beginning to open our eyes to new strategies for this present age. Jesus taught the people a new strategy for a new age that would bring them into new dimensions of intimacy and unforeseen power.

Ye have heard that it hath been said, Thou shalt love thy neighbour, and hate thine enemy. But I say unto you, Love your enemies, bless them that curse you, do good to them that hate you, and pray for them which despitefully use you, and persecute you; That ye may be the children of your Father which is in heaven: **Matt 5:43-45**

God, is more interested in our spiritual growth and development, than destroying our human enemies. The Wisdom of God is so far above our human wisdom that it's hard for us to see the value in blessing our enemies instead of cursing them. But, God's ultimate goal for his children is that we should be like him. We will rarely understand God's ways with our carnal/finite minds, and we will never become God's/Christ's likeness without the Holy Spirit. You see, we've got to desire the likeness of the Son of God, more than the darkness of the sons of men; the cup of blessing more than the cup of bitterness. Some of you may be thinking "I'm just not there", "They deserve to rot in hell for what they did to me or my loved one".

If it be possible, as much as lieth in you, live peaceably with all men. Dearly beloved, avenge not yourselves...

Romans 12:18-19

We have been called to a higher place in Christ, than the saints of old were called to under the Prophets. They were allowed to take an eye for an eye, but we are told not to avenge ourselves. But it doesn't stop there:

...but rather give place unto wrath: for it is written, Vengeance is mine; I will repay, saith the Lord....
Romans 12:19

It has been my experience that when I let the Lord fight my battles, and refuse to retaliate...He sends a much, much louder message to my enemies than I could ever send. This keeps my hands clean, and I can go on being the child of God that I am called to be.

Therefore if thine enemy hunger, feed him; if he thirst, give him drink: for in so doing thou shalt heap coals of fire on his head. Be not overcome of evil, but overcome evil with good.
Romans 12:20-21

Please pray this sample prayer of deliverance to break any strongholds that may exist within your soul or heart. Holy Spirit we ask you to lead us in this prayer and anoint every Word with power!

PRAYER:

Lord I reject (name it/them_____) and surrender my life fully to your will and plan for me In the name of the Lord Jesus Christ, by the Power of the Holy Spirit. I repent of my rebellion against your will and ways, and ask you to give me a clean heart. Lord, I ask you to heal every wound, and scar in my soul that has dominated my emotions and filled me with ungodly thoughts. Lord, take dominion and authority over every and any stronghold operating in my life (name it/them_____) Holy Spirit, I ask you to take absolute control of my life and have your way in me. Lord wash me and renew my hunger for your Truth, your Word is Truth...Your Truth has made me free! ...Amen

attend to my words; *Proverbs 4:19-21-***note page**

attend to my words; <u>Proverbs 4:19-21</u>**-note page**

Bitterness Part 2: Cancelling Emotional Debts

Behold, for peace I had great bitterness: but thou hast in love to my soul delivered it from the pit of corruption: for thou hast cast all my sins behind thy back. **Isaiah 38:17(KJV)**

Bitterness, here, is called a "pit of corruption" to the soul. Like a bitter grape is to the mouth,... bitterness sours the soul . When a person bites into a bitter grape, it is virtually impossible to hide the sour faced expression of displeasure. The Root of bitterness is often, but not always, visible within the personality of those affected by it. Because of the close relationship between bitterness and unforgiveness, this root not only has emotional implications, but spiritual and physical ones as well.

This root of bitterness usually enters the soul gradually, if given time to grow it will strangle the joy and happiness that we all need to balance out these trying times that we live in. Every person experiences bitterness to some degree, but when coupled with unforgiveness, bitterness can take a premiere place in the soul and begin to rule over all the emotions. It can become a Dominating Emotion.

Bitterness and unforgiveness cannot live in *a forgiving heart*, the choice to forgive is a decision made in obedience to Christ, who enabled us to be forgiven through the blood of His

Cross. The debt that we owed to God, before receiving Christ, was more than any could possibly pay. But God forgave this enormous debt, because Jesus paid the Death Penalty that we all deserved.

For the wages of sin is death; but the gift of God is eternal life through Jesus Christ our Lord. **Romans 6:23**

It is this truth, when it is revealed to our hearts, that makes us free from bitterness and unforgiveness against others. When we choose to forgive, grace and mercy are released within us and enable us to acquire a more forgiving heart. As we continue to yield to this work of God in our hearts we will soon experience the true freedom and healing that Christ came to give us.

Remember, forgiveness is a shield against bitterness. It was our Lord and Savior Jesus Christ that exemplified this best on the way to The Cross.

Then said Jesus, Father, forgive them; for they know not what they do. And they parted his raiment, and cast lots. And the people stood beholding. And the rulers also with them derided him, saying, He saved others; let him save himself, if he be Christ, the chosen of God. And the soldiers also mocked him, coming to him, and offering him vinegar, **Luke 23:34-36**

Jesus was fixed on Forgiveness ...He was willing to

Suffer the Bill (or payment for their sins) no matter what the cost!

"Forgive us our Debts, as we forgive our Debtors"
Matthew 6:12 (KJV)

How many emotional I.O. U.'s do you have to collect on?

I have met many women and men who have gone through divorces, or been the victims of adultery that carried emotional I.O.U.'s for many years after their marriages ended. These I.O.U.'s only served as reminders of the emotional price they paid during their marriages. Some, after years of separation were still waiting for their mates to redeem them emotionally by:

- Owning up to their wrongdoing
- and in some cases the women where waiting for validation from and reconciliation to husbands who would finally realized that they had left the best thing that had ever happened to them.

While this does happen occasionally, most often these emotional I.O.U.'s go unpaid and bitterness takes root over the process of time. Cancelling an emotional debt breaks the cycle of pain, shame and rejection, and allows for the heart to be healed and truly opened again to love, and be loved.

Owe no man any thing, but to love one another: for he that loveth another hath fulfilled the law. **Romans 13:8**

If there is a person that you have taken an emotional I.O.U. from, it's time to tear up the slip.

God loves our souls, and because he loves us, He's ready to walk us out of the place of bitterness. Now is the time for true freedom. Now is the time for Healing. This is your moment, embrace it! Won't you pray this prayer of forgiveness and freedom from bitterness:

PRAYER:

Father God I declare before your Holy Presence that I am ready to forgive and release every person from every emotional debt owed to me. I tear up and discard every emotional I.O.U. and release the memory of those debts unto you. Further more, I ask you Lord to forgive me for walking in bitterness, unforgiveness and resentment. I accept your matchless Grace in the full pardoning of my sins, as I forgive others who have trespassed against me. Lord I ask you to keep me free from the influence of bitterness as I will also be diligent to protect my heart from all forms of Satanic influence. Thank you Lord for your unconditional Love for me as I transition into the free and healing power of true forgiveness….Amen

attend to my words; <u>Proverbs 4:19-21</u>***-note page***

attend to my words; *Proverbs 4:19-21*-**note page**

Despising The Shame
(The Fear of Nakedness)

We need to be more Christ conscious today. It would save us a lot of emotional trouble. God's love, power and glory are <u>**a covering**</u> (and a hope) for mankind. Nothing else ever really works!.

There are so many ways to hide the shame. Some of us have been hiding for years. As the inner bondage to shame steals our freedom to live out in the open, we peek through the blinds of our lives presuming that we are well hidden, when in actuality many of us are painfully exposed as a running and hurting tribe of wanderers seeking asylum from our past hurts, failures and abuses. And unfortunately, Like Adam and Eve, we've been running away from the one who can restore us (His Image Upon Us). His Glory, Power and Presence!

And they heard the voice of the Lord God walking in the garden in the cool of the day: and Adam and his wife hid themselves from the presence of the Lord God amongst the trees of the garden. And the Lord God called unto Adam, and said unto him, Where art thou? And he said, I heard thy voice in the garden, and I was afraid, because I was naked; and I hid myself.

Genesis 3:8-10(KJV)

Our enemy, Satan, uses shame as a tool of separation and self-rejection. Shame is another DOMINATING EMOTION and

Spiritual Root for which the Word of God has an antidote:

> *...hope maketh not ashamed; because the love of God is shed abroad in our hearts by the Holy Ghost*
>
> **Romans 5:5**

Our Hope can easily be restored when a renewed vision of Jesus Christ is revealed within our hearts, for Jesus is and was the demonstrated Love of God, and it is through the wonderful Comforter, who is the Holy Ghost, that God's love (most visibly expressed through the offering of His Son) is shed abroad (as light shining in a dark place) throughout the caverns of our hearts, healing and holding our most inner and wounded parts. Let's allow the precious Holy Spirit to guide us through the processes of restoration from shame outlined in Romans chapter 5:1-5…

(This is my paraphrase of Romans 5:1-5)

Therefore being justified (declared not-guilty) by faith, we have inherited a peace treaty with God and are now standing in Grace, (God's Loving Favor, as His very own sons) rejoicing in hope of the Glory (the transforming power) of God's (presence) which allows us to Glory (Praise and be Changed) in tribulations for the working of Patience; and the working or gaining of experience; and the processing or establishing of REAL HOPE (with DIVINE properties); and the banishing and removal of ALL SHAME (rooted in Spiritual Nakedness and Self-Rejection), because of THE REVEALING OF GOD's LOVE IN OUR

HEARTS (AS A FLOOD-LIGHT) BY THE HOLY GHOST!

The Church of Laodicea appeared to have it all together on the surface,...They said "I am rich and increased with goods, and have need of nothing"...**Rev. 3:17** This is clearly an indication of spiritual blindness in the heart, but the Fire of Love in Jesus' eyes exposed their deepest and truest needs and the ACTUAL condition of this Church...Amongst those things revealed to them, Jesus exposes the **SHAME of their nakedness**, and counsels them to buy "White Raiment":

I counsel thee to buy of me gold tried in the fire, that thou mayest be rich; and white raiment, that thou mayest be clothed, and that ***the shame of thy nakedness do not appear****; and anoint thine eyes with eyesalve, that thou mayest see.*

Revelation 3:18

There was a condition of "Spiritual Nakedness" highlighted here, which brought them into a place of shame...This Shame was not the Dominating Emotion (emotionally they seemed to have it all together), but the Spiritual Root....

The Root of Shame is simply the manifestation of Spiritual Nakedness within or upon an Individual or Church...

What is Spiritual Nakedness, you might ask? It is the absence of God's presence upon/within a life, and the security that it (He) brings.

The Lord offers them a three fold cure...the First was to buy of him gold, which speaks of paying the price to recover his presence again in their lives... They would then have to perceive the value of his presence, and make a decision. Whatever the cost, in prayer, in repentance, in surrender, it would be worth it! Much like the Young Rich Ruler in Mark Chapter 10.

Then Jesus beholding him loved him, and said unto him, One thing thou lackest: go thy way, sell whatsoever thou hast, and give to the poor, and thou shalt have treasure in heaven: and come, take up the cross, and follow me. And he was sad at that saying, and went away grieved: for he had great possessions.

Mark 10:21-22

There are very few things with the power to seduce and blind the human heart like the pursuit of worldly riches. This undoubtedly is ybuy white raiment, which speaks of repentance and cleansing, Secondly he suggest they anoint their eyes with eyeslave, this speaks of healing the root of their spiritual nakedness, which was spiritual blindness (which they were not aware of). And thirdly Shame therefore begins as a Spiritual Root and then may be experienced as a **DOMINATING EMOTION.**

When Adam sinned, the Spiritual Root of Shame was sown in Him and it manifested as **"The Fear of nakedness"**...The putting on of a fig leaf was not a remedy for Shame, only a hiding place from shame...Of course, it is impossible to hide from a spiritual root that has been sown in your own being, ….   We often put things on (fig leaves) in an attempt to keep others from seeing our spiritual state of being...In a sense we are adding layers of activities, addictions, appetites and accessories to our outer lives, but to no avail, because the problem lies within us, in the core of our being, where surrender happens, and forgiveness is realized, and intimacy is consummated. It's only at the place of encounter with God that this Spiritual Root of Shame is cursed, and withers, never again to bear fruit in our lives.

The Word "buy" (Rev 3:18) here means to purchase or redeem...or to pay the price to obtain something...Well, the truth is that trusting in their carnal riches made them "Spiritually Poor" (ignorant of the need for The True Riches, The Riches of His Glory, and the Full Inheritance of Spiritual Blessings in Christ Jesus), not to be confused with being "poor in spirit"(a place of realizing our need for God) which has great benefits. They could only purchase this "White Raiment" if they abandoned "not their riches", but "trusting in their riches", and not in the Precious Blood of the Lamb which is the agent that washes away our sins.

And I said unto him, Sir, thou knowest. And he said to me, These are they which came out of great tribulation, and have washed their robes, and <u>made them white in the blood of the Lamb</u>. **Revelation 7:14**

Trusting in ANYTHING other than the Wealth of God's Kingdom and it's Riches amounts to blindness and nakedness which will lead to shame. Buy the GOLD, Buy the Gold, Buy the Gold through a Poverty of Spirit (the understanding that He alone can satisfy the longing in our hearts) which often makes one Rich in Faith, in looking unto to Jesus "The Author and the Finisher of our Faith"

...Judas betrayed Jesus for Thirty pieces of Silver, God is not impressed by our earthly wealth...He owns the cattle on a thousand hills, and the streets of Heaven are paved with Gold....once again,...He is not impressed...He is looking for those who are looking for Him!

And they were both naked, the man and his wife, and were not ashamed. **Genesis 2:25**

Before sin entered into the picture mankind knew no shame. There was a freedom that accompanied our state of innocence. The influence of evil stole this shameless state and brought in a new state of being...self-consciousness. Once our eyes were opened to "the knowledge of evil" by eating from that tree (see Genesis Ch. 3), **we saw ourselves (in the mirror of self-**

consciousness), and the world around us, in a whole new light. We were now prohibited from looking upon each other because of this new influence of evil.

Sin steals Glory, Glory (Light) displaces Darkness, Blood covers Sin... PAPER, ROCK, SCISSORS

This new influence made us feel ashamed. It effectively stripped us of our spiritual covering (the image of God), and exposed us as fallen humanity (having lost our innocence). There was a clear connection between what happened in our hearts and how we felt about our bodies and our inner selves.

And the eyes of them both were opened, and they knew that they were naked; and they sewed fig leaves together, and made themselves aprons.

Genesis 3:7 (KJV)

Hiding is a natural response to feeling ashamed...Just as these aprons failed to free them from their shame, so do our fig leaves (wardrobes, religious or educational accomplishments, bank statements, associations, cliques, vices, addictions, heavy make-up etc.) fail to free us from our shame...

Shame is more than an emotional response, shame can be a spiritual root like that of bitterness which can lodge deep within the human soul. Shame is the magnified consciousness of self in the face of judgment for weakness, frailty or failure. Shame is a product of separation from God, it is the reality of what we have lost because of what we or someone else has done. Shame had no place in Adam and Eve before sin because they were not self-conscious, they were not separated from God. They were so spiritual, they didn't even know that they were naked. They were clothed by God Himself.

And He said, who told thee that thou wast naked?

Genesis 3:11 a

Sin handed them a Mirror!

Put that mirror down and pick up the mirror of God's Love...It is a talking mirror, and it speaks very highly of you!

Shame has no power to resist this powerful antidote. It kills Shame from the very root, repairing the heart and function of the soul. God's Love repairs our vision... getting our eyes off of ourselves, and putting our eyes back where they belong...On The Almighty God. Who saves, Who forgives, Who heals, restores and sets free!

Jesus is the Rock, He Shed the Blood, and He Died on the Tree (Paper)

Jesus is the way to the Father, the Holy Spirit is the gift of the Son, and he brings this Amazing Love into our hearts. If you don't know Jesus as your personal Savior and Lord, just turn to the last page of this book and pray that prayer with an open heart; then return here and ask the Holy Spirit to fill your heart with this amazing love. It may even happen spontaneously after you receive Jesus into your hearts.

attend to my words; <u>Proverbs 4:19-21</u>*-note page*

attend to my words; <u>Proverbs 4:19-21</u>*-note page*

Rejection

What is a root of rejection? A root of rejection is a deep seated emotional wound usually caused by the refusal, denial or dismissal of someone by another person that is beloved or ***deeply connected*** to them, even in the unborn. A root of rejection can also be caused by a series of negative responses over a period of time. It is also possible for this root to take place through a demonic attack against the heart and soul.

What ever the cause of a person's experience with rejection, he or she will almost assuredly be confronted by a Spirit of Rejection (a demonic foe). The agenda of the Spirit of Rejection is to use rejections pain as a tool for the kingdom of darkness. I believe that Satan himself suffers from this wound of rejection, and seeks to inflict others with this pain. His rejection was preceded by self-delusion, the delusion of victory in a war against God. This was extraordinary deception, and because he believed in his quest and desired to be equal with and/or above God, when his plan failed, an extraordinary wound of rejection was formed. The deception presented to Adam and Eve was born from Satan's own sense of Rejection.

And the serpent said unto the woman, Ye shall not surely die: For God doth know that in the day ye eat thereof, then your eyes shall be opened, and ye shall be as gods, knowing good and evil. **Genesis 3:4-5**

Satan, here, is trying to convince Eve of the same deceptive lie that got him cast out of Heaven. That she could be equal to, or ***as*** God by disobeying Him. He would later solidify this connection between rejection and deception when he offered our Lord Jesus Christ the Kingdoms of this world.

And the devil, taking him up into an high mountain, shewed unto him all the kingdoms of the world in a moment of time. And the devil said unto him, All this power will I give thee, and the glory of them: for that is delivered unto me; and to whomsoever I will I give it. If thou therefore wilt worship me, all shall be thine. And Jesus answered and said unto him, Get thee behind me, Satan: for it is written, Thou shalt worship the Lord thy God, and him only shalt thou serve. **Luke 4:5-8**

Here the devil is asking the Son of God to bow down and worship him, in exchange for this worlds kingdoms. He is clearly still seeking to be Lord, to be as God, to be like or equal to God. But Jesus, addresses this deception boldly.

"Thou shalt worship the Lord thy God, and him only shalt thou serve." **Luke 4:8**

In other words, Jesus was saying...STOP DECIEVING YOURSELF! We must be careful that we do not embrace rejections traits, just because we have been a victim of rejections pain. **Deception is the author of much of humanity's tragedy...**

3 Things the deceiver uses to traumatize humanity

1.) Broken Homes producing

Rejections, Abandonments, Divorces, Infidelities, Affairs, Physical, Emotional and Verbal Abuse, Molestations, Condemnation etc.

2.) Broken Marriages/Relationships producing

Self-rejection, Condemnation, Failure, Unworthiness, Depression, Rejection, Unforgiveness, Self-pity, Unwillingness to move on, Propensity to look back, Invalidation

3.) Broken Relationship with God...

Like Adam and Eve of old, so many precious believers have allowed shame to keep them from returning to the Lord. What you may be ashamed of now, God is so willing to forgive and heal. **The Blood of Jesus Christ cleanses us from all sin. Run into the arms of a loving Father. His mercies are new every morning. Ask him to forgive you because of the precious Blood of Jesus...He is more than Willing!**

The enemy devotes many of his efforts towards unsettling the security of God's Children today through deceptions. He is infamous for assaulting God's people with hounding temptations and then returning to them with cynical condemnations when they fall. **DECLARE THIS WITH ME: "Shame and self-rejection...I let you go"**

Rejections pain can become a launching pad from which all men may slide into the snares of temporal acceptance by seeking money, power, drugs, lust and many other vices in an attempt to fill the void in them. Satan's use of rejection as a tool is a by-product of his failed attempt to trump God. Rejection's purpose is to eliminate purpose and eradicate hope. I call this a tool because it can be used to control and enslave. I once met a man who used rejection as a tool against women. By initially rejecting them, he caused many women to seek his approval and acceptance that much more...This tool was born from the bosom of the enemy.

Self-rejection and self-abuse are often the result when a person concedes to rejection as a master, and agrees with it's voice. This is a common strategy of the Serpent (the Devil). He uses this venom to reduce the resistance of a person to his will. And then he attempts to make them a captive to it (his will).

This bite (attack) of the serpent can leave a painful wound. One of the most serious wounds is Rejection.

While shame hides..., rejection on the other hand continues to seek validation (love) in all the wrong places, in hopes of acceptance. It is this seeking that makes those who struggle with rejection so vulnerable. The root of rejection runs deep and can interweave within a persons heart and soul. Our Lord Jesus Christ was despised and rejected of men. He was touched with the feelings of our infirmities. His love is the antidote for rejections' venom. When Jesus rose in victory from the dead, we were risen with Him. Rejection was crushed under His feet for you and for me! Jesus was despised and rejected of **men**, ***but he never embraced the root of rejection***. He never became a root of rejection, because he was accepted, sent and approved by God, his Father. Jesus had been inoculated with the love of God, and rejection is no match for God's LOVE.

...For this purpose the Son of God was manifested, that he might destroy the works of the devil. **I John 3:8**

A deep root

The Lord wants to go deep...I can hear this song in my spirit. "I wanna go deep, I wanna go deep, and when I go deep, I'm gonna Heal Deep, I'm gonna Heal you Deeply..."

His love kills rejection's root and frees our hearts and souls to trust, to love, to feel , and to live again. We have looked for acceptance in relationships, through yielding to immoral sexual activity, we have paid for love, been cheated and manipulated, used and abused, conned and corralled, only to find ourselves exhausted and unfulfilled. It's time to reject rejection!

The good news is that there is one who is worthy of our pursuit, and yet he seeks no gift at all. No, it's you that he wants, it's you he came to save. You are the apple of his eye. Look up, look into his eyes...there's not an ounce of rejection within them... There's a fire of love burning towards you (...and his eyes *were* as a flame of fire **Rev 1:14**)...Let it melt your heart, and burn away the chains of rejection. He will never hurt you as others have done. He is love. He is the Truth. He is the real thing.

DECLARE THIS OUT LOUD: Rejection, I let you GO! Jesus I let you IN. Heal me Lord. Go deep... I'm ready to be revived. I'm ready to be restored...

You may be thinking "I've done too much, gone too far, my life is over," no, no, no, Life is too precious to think that way...That's what the serpent wants you to believe. But don't listen to his lies. Maybe your saying: "I pray", "I believe in Jesus", "I do all of that" ...almost everybody that I've heard say that, was living for God on their own terms...I challenge you to come as you are and give God your all...Let's take a good look at our own hearts.

Those of us who have been rejected, are often guilty of rejecting the Love of Jesus? Have you been rejecting the call of Jesus Christ to a greater commitment to Him.

If so, say those words again...

"Rejection I let you GO, Jesus I let you IN"

Here comes a new wave of God's love

quenching the fires of rejection.

If you have given Jesus your heart, but still haven't come into that place of true freedom from rejection. Take a look back at your spiritual notes and see if you've walked out in obedience to the known will of God for your life. God calls us Higher, Deeper, and into the Ever-Narrowing pathways of His Eternal Kingdom. His Love, Power and Glory will strip rejections power as we follow the Lamb wherever he leads. Look into His Love...Gaze into His eyes...Worship the Lord in the beauty of Holiness...Fall at His feet and wash them in your tears...Mop them with your hair...Let the Glory of God shower down upon you as you magnify the Son...The reign of rejection of over...The rule of the Kingdom is here...Surrender to God's Love...it's casting out all of your fears...SING a song from your heart…become the melody...the instrument...pour out your soul unto Him...He's waiting for you...He's waiting for you…

The pain of your rejection is no match for the Love of God.
Receive this prayer: In Jesus authority

I break every ungodly soul tie to every person or event that has hurt you. I release you into the arms of Love and bind you, heart to heart, to the bosom of Jesus Christ. As you sink deeper into the cleft of his heart and love for you, there's but one thing for you to do...Lean on your beloved, Lean on your beloved. Say this with me: Jesus, I lean on your love, I lean on your love.

attend to my words; <u>Proverbs 4:19-21</u>*-note page*

attend to my words; <u>Proverbs 4:19-21</u>*-note page*

Pride and Corruption (Part 1)

Without God (Who is Ingenerate (Reproducing Itself Eternally) Love and Life), the knowledge of good and/or evil can wreak havoc on the ill-prepared...Adam was warned by God not to eat from that tree! Only God could consume (know intimately) good and evil and not be consumed (known intimately) by good and evil. Without wisdom, knowledge gets short-circuited... God created all things by faith, which works by love, only He can rightly handle his creations, because He alone knows what He has in mind for His creations...Adam and Eve were not yet prepared to handle the "knowledge" of good and evil when they ate from the tree. They would not have become as God through knowledge alone, as the Serpent told them...Though they were created in the image and likeness of God, they were not equal with God in terms of all of His attributes...They were not ready to handle, control or rightly divide all knowledge...

Man has built many systems based upon knowledge that have failed for lack of wisdom....God had the Wisdom, but they failed to seek His counsel. And without Love (God), they "profited nothing". Love gives efficacy and application to knowledge, it gives life, but "the letter killeth" without wisdom. God's Wisdom gives quality, it gives substance, and it protects against corruption. Pride is the result of corruption...which is a by-product of lust. Satan (Lucifer) looked at the Glory of GOD, and said to himself...I want some of that...I gotta have it, no matter what, I gotta get it. SATAN HAD NO USE FOR PAPER MONEY IN HEAVEN...***GOD'S GLORY*** WAS HIS DESIRE, WHAT HE LUSTED AFTER, MORE THAN ANYTHING....

When his heart was filled with Envy and Pride, he began to recruit one third of the angels into this darkness, into this Lust for MONEY/GLORY. He was controlling them and they didn't even know it. As these corrupted angels became just like him, they also began to lust for MONEY/GLORY. He sold the worst drug to ever hit the streets of Heaven...No it wasn't Crack, Meth or Dust...it was THE LOVE OF MONEY/SELF/GLORY.

Note: Of course we know that God will not share His Glory. This being said, if Satan could have somehow wrestled the Glory away from God, it would have destroyed him instantly. Considering this, perhaps this is one of the reasons why God does not give us everything we ask for. Because they would destroy us.

*By your **corrupt** ways of doing business, you defiled your holy places of worship.* **Ezekiel 28 The Message**

He kept looking at GOD..., looking at GOD...and before he knew it...,he wanted to BE GOD. Then he served this drug called PRIDE to heavens community of angels, and one out of three got addicted to it. Satan and his wicked angels were Cast Out of Heaven. He has been selling THIS PRIDE DRUG in the Earth for ages. This is his CORRUPT BUSINESS... Satan is the

Biggest Drug Dealer on the Planet. It is the PRIDE of Life, that Produces the Love of Money...which is the ROOT of all evil!

PRAYER: Lord, I pray, that we your people would become highly sensitive to the prevailing influence of evil targeting the conscience of man in these last days. Help us to erect the Gate of Truth over our mental and physical loins, and live as free men and women in this corrupt world.

DECLARATION: I GIRD UP THE LOINS OF MY MIND IN THE NAME OF JESUS CHRIST AND HOPE TO THE END FOR THE GRACE THAT IS COMING TO ME AS FRESH REVELATION/MANIFESTATION FROM JESUS (THE WORD OF LIFE). DIRECTING, STRENGTHENING, ENLIGHTENING, EMPOWERING, EXPOSING EVERY LYING STRATEGY OF THE ENEMY, BRINGING ME INTO YOUR COMPLETE PROVIDENCE AND OVERCOMING PURPOSES FOR MY LIFE.

attend to my words; <u>Proverbs 4:19-21</u>*-note page*

attend to my words; *Proverbs 4:19-21*-**note page**

Modern Day Corrupters (Pride and Division)

*Beloved, my whole concern was to write to you in regard to our common salvation. [But] I found it necessary and was impelled to write you and urgently appeal to and exhort [you] to contend for the faith which was once for all [a]handed down to the saints [the faith which is that sum of Christian belief which was delivered [b]verbally to the holy people of God]. ⁴ For certain men have crept in stealthily [[c]gaining entrance secretly by a side door]. Their doom was predicted long ago, ungodly (impious, profane) persons who **pervert the grace** (the spiritual blessing and favor) of our God into lawlessness and wantonness and immorality, and disown and deny our sole Master and Lord, Jesus Christ (the Messiah, the Anointed One).* **Jude 1:3-4 Amp**

Heaven's community of angels corrupted through the influence of Pride and Envy

⁵Now I want to remind you, though you were fully informed once for all, that though the Lord [at one time] delivered a people out of the land of Egypt, He subsequently destroyed those [of them] who did not believe [who refused to adhere to, trust in, and rely upon Him].⁶ And angels who did not keep (care for,

guard, and hold to) their own first place of power but abandoned their proper dwelling place—these He has reserved in custody in eternal chains (bonds) under the thick gloom of utter darkness until the judgment *and* doom of the great day. ⁷[The wicked are sentenced to suffer] just as Sodom and Gomorrah and the adjacent towns—which likewise gave themselves over to impurity and indulged in unnatural vice *and* sensual perversity—are laid out [in plain sight] as an exhibit of perpetual punishment [to warn] of everlasting fire. ⁸Nevertheless in like manner, these dreamers also corrupt the body, scorn *and* reject authority *and* government, and revile *and* libel *and* scoff at [heavenly] glories (the glorious ones). **Jude 1:5-10 Amp**

Pride has a history of corruption and subsequent judgment! It also stands today, as perhaps the most corrupt and dominating emotion there is. We can clearly see from these passages of scripture, that pride leads a very destructive path as it deceives, corrupts and exalts itself... We must defend ourselves against this Dominating Emotion/Spiritual Root at all costs. The Holy nature of God has the power to purge out the influence of this spiritual predator called pride, because centered within God's very nature there is a Holy Love that knows no pride...

Whereby are given unto us exceeding great and precious promises: that by these ye might be partakers of the divine nature, having escaped the corruption that is in the world through lust.
2 Peter 1:4

Believer's today can escape the corruption that pride and lust bring, by partaking of God's own nature. We become partakers when we are indwelled by the Holy Spirit. The Holy Spirit is the Divine Nature of God, and very God Himself. The Divine Nature of God is Holy. It is through the abiding presence of the Holy Spirit upon and within us, that we are changed from Glory to Glory. His gentle hands at work in our lives, teaching, guiding, helping, convicting, and prompting us towards real freedom as we yield to this new nature.

attend to my words; <u>Proverbs 4:19-21</u>*-note page*

attend to my words; <u>Proverbs 4:19-21</u>*-note page*

Pride again

For all that is in the world, the lust of the flesh, and the lust of the eyes, and the pride of life, is not of the Father, but is of the world. **1John 2:16**

Pride is so lifted by it's own arrogance that it denies it's own need for help. Pride is the fullness of deception, and is a major cause of spiritual blindness! I'm not addicted, I can stop anytime I want to, I'm not drunk. I'm not afraid... If I had a job, a wife, a husband, etc. my life would be...

This dominating emotion often arises out of a recurring sense of failure or helplessness, or any one of the previously mentioned dominating emotions. It can also arise out of a sense of success or accomplishment. All of us have some pride in one area of our lives or another. There are some who deny that they have any pride at all, but this is pride in its purest form. Because pride is a root sin, it expresses itself in many ways and comes in many colors, as a myriad of leaves on an autumn tree. Denials, disasters, deceptions and many devilish delusions have sprung forth from this root of Pride.

One evening after praying for a friend at a local Hospital, I happened to look into the room of an older man as I was leaving the floor. When our eyes met, he cried out loud to me more than once. I immediately felt to minister healing to the man, and walked into his room to ask him if I could pray for him. Though he seemed to cry out in desperation, His reply was… "No you can't pray for me, I don't need nobody to pray for me, I can pray for myself" "I know how to pray, I can pray for myself" He apparently wanted my company, but not my prayers…So I waited patiently to see if there was something else I could do for him, and while he may have wanted me to be there, his every statement was pushing me away.

I could see that there was great pride within this man, who was very strong in his convictions, and had a very strong physical frame. This was not a boasting pride or a braggadocios pride, but a pride born from a sense of loss, a sense of helplessness, where this once strong man found himself in an unfamiliar place of need.

As I conceded not to pray for him, and began to walk out of the door, I spoke a few kind words to him as I was leaving, and he emphatically replied "You're not praying for me are you, I can pray for myself, I don't need nobody to pray for me, you're not praying for me are you"???

Pride can keep us from receiving God's best. I used to walk in this area of pride myself. I could give you the shirt off of my back, but found it very hard to receive from others…This went on until I realized the losses I had suffered at the hands of my own pride.

…for without me ye can do nothing. **John 15:5**

All pride is not equal

Pride is not always a sign of arrogance or a sense of superiority, rather, it can often be the result of incomplete yieldedness in times of trial. I call this defensive pride. You may have heard the saying "all I have left is my pride". For some, pride has become their last great possession. Perhaps after a series of losses or a humiliating event, a divorce, or the loss a job, some cleave to the Rock of Pride. The problem is that Pride doesn't translate into Power. At best, it remains as a substitute for power, a box of emotional quicksand, sinking us deeper and deeper into self. Where pride may offer excuses for our troubles, God's Power offers solutions to our troubles. When self-pity and pride join forces within the human personality, they form a nearly impenetrable bond of concrete around the heart and mind. These two dominating emotions are from the same family of emotional strongholds.

The Family of I-motions.

Whereas Self-Pity may say "I don't deserve any help", Pride may say "I don't need any help", even when the person really does. In both cases there is a need for a breakthrough to cry out to Jesus. To press beyond these emotional shackles called pride and self-pity, without regard for who's looking at us, or how many times we've failed to see the hand of God. Or the length of time we have been in a particular state of being. Our Lord Jesus Christ encountered many that had endured long-term afflictions. The one that comes to mind is that of the woman with the issue of blood. She would have been a clear candidate for self-pity and defensive pride. It wasn't until she had experienced many failures, that she saw Jesus in the press, touched the hem of his garment, and was made completely whole. This daughter of Abraham refused to allow pride to steal her miracle!

And, behold, a woman which was diseased with an issue of blood twelve years, came behind him, and touched the hem of his garment: for she said within herself, If I may but touch his garment I shall be whole. But Jesus turned him about, and when he saw her, he said, Daughter, be of good comfort; thy faith hath made thee whole. **Matthew 9:20-21**

Her issue of blood would have been a stigma in those days, declaring her ceremonially unclean and unfit for contact with other people. Yet, despite this obstacle, she had tunnel-vision. The crowds couldn't dissuade her. The noise didn't distract her. She girt up the loins of her mind, sobered her thoughts and declared her plan within herself. "If I may but touch the hem of his garment"...This was clearly an example of a woman who "hoped 'til the end for the grace". There was not another example in scripture of a miracle happening by touching the hem of a garment. Grace brought the Revelation of Jesus Christ. Yes, I believe that the Holy Spirit revealed the method by which she could be healed, and she obeyed the revelation. Whatever you do beloved, obey the revelation!

attend to my words; <u>Proverbs 4:19-21</u>*-note page*

attend to my words; <u>Proverbs 4:19-21</u>*-note page*

Self-Pity

Self-Pity is like a cage that opens and closes from the inside. When a person is overcome by this Dominating Emotion, they can become their own worst enemy. Many who struggle with Self-Pity embrace the present condition, whether it is true or false, with a sense of submission and surrender. Every one has battled with this at some point in their lives, but if a person remains in this state of mind, hopelessness (a state of emotional distress, despair and depression) can soon overtake them, and a sense of total defeat can set in. **Why me**, often becomes the whole focus, causing opportunities for freedom and deliverance to go unnoticed.

Self Pity may display itself dramatically at times, in order to enlist the attention of others, and of course, we should be attentive to the hurting among us, all the while encouraging them to focus on the solution, the answer, the open door. My wife often says, "you don't know if you don't feel". Self-pity often invites others into it's cage for a "pity party"...and there can come a sense of temporary relief in knowing that someone else is feeling your pain. The problem with this is that self-pity hinders the healing process. Once healing begins and freedom increases, self-pity desires to bring us back to the most painful parts of our experiences in order to gain sympathy and understanding. In other words, self-pity fosters defeat. No matter how good it feels to wallow in Self-Pity, it's still holding off the true lasting victory and deliverance that God has in store for us. The remedy for Self-Pity is getting up and going forth.

And there were four leprous men at the entering in of the gate: and they said one to another, Why sit we here until we die?

2Kings 7:3

There was a famine amongst the people of God, and conditions in Samaria were very desperate...These four lepers had three options as they stood at the gate; (1) To go forward into a famine (into the city of Samaria)...(2) To stay where they were and die or (3) To go head first into the enemies camp (outside of the city) in hopes of staying alive. This was a determined act of faith. They did not wait for self-pity to set in. In addition to their leprosy, they were in the middle of a life threatening conflict. But, when they went into the enemies camp, the Lord had caused there enemies to scatter before them!!! Hallelujah!!!

When it seems like there's no hope, remember that the Lord goes before you, and He's never lost a battle!!! If they had not made the choice to get up, get going and address their fears, they would have died unnecessarily.

Moving out of Self-Pity requires a decided effort to get going. [It must be understood that self-pity has great influence within the realm of the soul because of painful memories both past and present, you may have to build up your spirit on the word of God and prayer, to gain strength to move forward in victory]. I can't think of any substance more motivating than the Word of God.

And David was greatly distressed; for the people spake of stoning him, because the soul of all the people was grieved, every man for his sons and for his daughters: but David encouraged himself in the LORD his God. **1Samuel 30:6**

This would have been a perfect opportunity for David to wallow in Self-Pity, but instead, David remembered the Lord! David most assuredly encouraged himself with the promises of God, and his very own personal experiences with God's protection. God's Word is full of promises of protection, provision, healing and deliverance for His children. When Self-Pity tries to set in, run to your Father and to His Word! Keep a journal of even the smallest of victories. The tiniest of interventions. These are often the ones where we see God's power and love most clearly.

Bless the LORD, O my soul: and all that is within me, bless his holy name. Bless the LORD, O my soul, and forget not all his benefits: Who forgiveth all thine iniquities; who healeth all thy diseases; Who redeemeth thy life from destruction ... **Psalms 103:1-4a**

attend to my words; <u>Proverbs 4:19-21</u>**-note page**

attend to my words; *Proverbs 4:19-21*-**note page**

Fear
The Torment Trap

There is no fear in love; but perfect love casteth out fear: because fear hath torment. He that feareth is not made perfect in love. **1John 4:18**

These torments are not described in the scripture, but they could be likened to the various torturous interrogation techniques that have been used against prisoners of war to gain intelligence or information. These tortures or torments are used to break the will first, which makes the gathering of information much easier to attain. The human will is a force to be reckoned with though, when it is enforced by the knowledge of God's will (God's Word), and empowered by the Holy Spirit. It has the power to resist fear and overthrow every torment by deciding to stand firmly in faith upon God's Word. This combo of sword and shield will enable the Spirit to Fight while the Soul recovers.

When the spirit and soul have emerged from a battle with fear, and have stood with the remaining armor in tact (the Helmet of **Salvation**, the Breastplate of **Righteousness**, the Loins girt about with **Truth** and the Feet shod with the Preparation of the Gospel of **Peace**), preparation should be made for another round with this spiritual enemy. The preparation of the Gospel of Peace. Now the "Gospel of Peace" may sound like a non-violent, passive resistance, but biblically speaking peace has more than one dimension.*** (stay out of fears arena, resist the realm of reasoning's. If a stronghold has been built and occupied by a strongman...Perfect Love is still able to cast it out)

What is Love's Power over Fear, it is this...Perfect Love is the manifestation of The Almighty God in His purest and most accessible form (it's always available). It is the embodiment of God's Person. Fear runs from Perfect Love, because it has no power over it, no answer to it, no place of entry, access or influence. Fear needs access to function. It needs a point of reference, something to feed from in order to torment. Love gives fear no access...because there is no fear in Love...Love simply knows no fear... fear is powerless in the presence of Perfect Love. Perfect Love is not subject to the fall....so it is not subject to Fear...It is of Divine Quality, it is FEARLESS!

Fear is afraid of Love. Love is stronger than death. When the fear of death is conquered, we are divinely repositioned into a place of Power and Advantage. Love is the greatest untapped weapon amongst God's children...It is the most powerful substance in the Kingdom of God. It makes quick work of fear and every worker of darkness. Jesus was able to overcome the forces of hell itself in the Garden of Gethsemane as the weight of the worlds sin, and the powers of darkness assailed against his mind, will and emotions, but perfect love cast out fear. Perfect love conquered the fear of death. Perfect Love took the Sting out of death itself. Perfect love dispelled all darkness. The Devil can't stand the light, the light is a manifestation of Perfect Love. If we stay in the Light and In Love, we will always avoid the Torment Trap!

What is a Tormenting Spirit?

It is a demonic hound by nature, leaving only for short seasons and returning to look for evidence of it's effectiveness.

Endeavor not to allow the devil to get you focused on the things that you cannot control. This will only fuel his efforts to torment. (If we are looking at the things which we cannot control, we will soon run short on hope)

This is a KEY strategy of the enemy, and it is in this arena that "Imaginations" can run wild, feeding our minds false evidence appearing real. Get out of this ARENA...it is a TORMENT TRAP. Refuse to look at anything other than The Word of Truth!

Hope deferred makes the heart sick... **Proverbs 13:12**

I want you to see yourself right now walking out of the devil's arena, and into the Kingdom of God. The Kingdom of God is the Arena of Divine Possibility. The enemy must enter into your arena if he wants to wage a war against your soul. Declare this with me NOW "I am walking out of the arena of tormenting imaginations where there are things outside of my control, and I am walking into the arena of The Kingdom of God, where Righteousness, Peace and Joy in the Holy Ghost are continually accessible to me.

(A Great Resource for walking out of areas of captivity to fear is coming soon in my book "The Knowledge Trap": Three Dimensional Protection Against Fear". When something or someone is trying to hold you in bondage, or keep you from going forward, quite often fear is behind it. The fear of loss, the fear of change, the fear of being alone, the fear of failure, the fear of success, the fear of ridicule, the fear of confrontation and the fear of doom, are just a small sampling of ways in which the Spirit of Fear manifests in the human soul.

A NOTE ON THIS: Beware, when you move toward your freedom from fear, bondage and affliction, there may be those around you that will try to discourage your movement. The fear in them doesn't want to be alone. Fear loves company, and looks for friends to support itself.

If you cannot take others into the promise land of (REAL FREEDOM) with you, then you must distance yourself from the fearful. The Spirit of Fear is not from God, and can be contagious.

And Caleb stilled the people before Moses, and said, Let us go up at once, and possess it; for we are well able to overcome it. But the men that went up with him said, ***We be not able to go up against the people; for they are stronger than we.*** *And they brought up* ***an evil report*** *of the land which they had searched*

unto the children of Israel, saying, The land, through which we have gone to search it, is a land that eateth up the inhabitants thereof; and all the people that we saw in it are men of a great stature. **And there we saw the giants, the sons of Anak, which come of the giants:** *and we were in our own sight as grasshoppers, and so we were in their sight. And all the congregation lifted up their voice, and cried;* **and the people wept that night. :**
Numbers 13:30-14:2

The Spirit of Fear took hold in the camp because the fearful came back with an evil (fear based) report even though God promised them the Land. Caleb saw the same thing as the men that went up with him, and yet he was able to defeat fear and move forward. Caleb, undoubtedly knew God intimately. This kind of faith comes by hearing His voice, knowing His ways, and experiencing His Love. Fear cannot live in the presence of God.

There is no fear in love; but perfect love casteth out fear: because fear hath torment. He that feareth is not made perfect in love. **1John 4:18**

God's Love is perfect. It will arise and cover you. It will put out all of the fires. Who can stand before His presence? He's an awesome God, with an awesome heart of Love and Mercy... Intimacy, Intimacy, Intimacy with God quells the fires of fear, and rains in with truth, and rains in with trust, and rains in with life, and rains down Miracles, and Miracles and Miracles and Miracles…Abide in His presence and you will experience total freedom from Fear, and every other Dominating Emotion!

If you've gotten an evil (fear based) report, if there are giants in your life…
Call on your Heavenly Father…
He hears, He cares,
He's well able to get you to your promise land

attend to my words; <u>Proverbs 4:19-21</u>*-note page*

attend to my words; *Proverbs 4:19-21*-**note page**

The Dominion of Love

In some, but not all cases, demonization is at the root of certain dominating emotions, the more rooted they become, the more difficult it may be to attain complete freedom, depending on the elements of Faith, Power and Love.

Love is the most powerful Force in the Kingdom of God. It is pure, transferrable and healing in its function. This is the substance that flowed through Jesus Christ. He does everything by and through Love. His Rule and Kingdom are subject to Love for He is Love Himself.

Love has Breadth, Length, Height and Depth, each of these are Spiritual Dimensions. Each one of those dimensions is infinite in its capacity, and absolute in its integrity. Love like this is not of carnal or natural origin. It is a pure substance outflowing from the Holiness of God. If untempered, Love would consume us as easily as a raging, untamable fire. Only, this *Fire, is under Sovereign control.* Our God is a consuming fire, He is Love in its purest form, like a white flame, the hottest part of a fire. The Song of Solomon makes mention of this kind of Love.

Many waters cannot quench love, neither can the floods drown it: if a man would give all the substance of his house for love, it would utterly be contemned. **Song of Solomon 8:7**

To manifest this Love-Fire within, and offer it freely to

this dying world is a part of God's purpose for us. It is His Highest Design, His most desired attribute for His people. It has been my experience that this kind of Love only manifests in proportion to the level of brokenness manifested within a life. God pours His Love out most readily through broken vessels, onto other broken vessels, into other broken vessels...

If we were to meditate upon His Love for us, as often as we meditated upon the trials we face, we would engage the most powerful substance there is.

Therefore being justified by faith, we have peace with God through our Lord Jesus Christ. By whom we have access into this grace wherein we stand, and rejoice in hope of the glory of God. And not only so, but we glory in tribulations also: knowing that tribulation worketh patience; And patience, experience, and experience hope: And hope maketh not ashamed; **because the Love of God is shed abroad by the Holy Ghost which is given unto us.**
Romans 5:1-5

The Holy Spirit dispenses Love into our hearts as we are being processed through various trials...It (Love) is the antidote for every human illness., it is the balm for every injury, it is the remedy for every affliction, it is the foundation of every answer to every question. It is the ultimate destination, and the primary motive for all of God's intervention, expressly the Cross. It is the upward call to the Saint, the outward reach to the broken, and a complete mystery to the demonic ranks.

Love is both a Dominating Emotion and

A Spiritual Root

That Christ may dwell in your hearts by faith; that ye, being rooted and grounded in love, may be able to comprehend with all saints what is the breadth, and length, and depth and height; And to know the Love of Christ, which passeth knowledge, that ye may be filled with all the fullness of God. **Ephesians 3:17-19**

that ye, being rooted...

This is the first undertaking of love, the initial measure and understanding of Love...

and grounded in love...

This is the wrapping of those roots around your heart, having a firm foundation in Love

may be able to comprehend with all saints what is the breadth, and length, and depth and height; And to know the Love of Christ...

This is the place of first entering into the unimaginable depths, heights etc. of the Love carried by our Lord Jesus Christ

which passeth knowledge, that ye may be filled with all the fullness of God...

I BELIEVE This to be the Highest Calling there is...to know the love of Christ which passeth knowledge, that we may be filled with all the fullness of God...

This prayer, offered by the Apostle Paul, shows the complete and total desire of God our Father for us to be partakers of His divine nature, His fullness, His power, Freedom and Love! Fear, Bitterness, Shame, Rejection, Pride and Self-Pity could never survive in an internal environment such as this. They can't live in the presence of genuine Love. Spending time praying this prayer over ourselves will effectively draw us into the depths, heights, the breadths and Lengths of His remarkable Love.

Believer's Prayer:

Father, I ask that you would enable me to be rooted and grounded, making me stable and sure footed in Love, so that I can understand and experience, with all of your children, the liberating depths, breadths, length's and heights of your Steadfast Love, which go way beyond human understanding and knowledge, that I may know and actually be touched and filled with the Love of Christ in my deepest depths, which is beyond the capacity of intellect or reason, that I may be irrefutably filled with all the fullness of you, bringing me rest and complete freedom from the dominion of every Dominating Emotion!

Prayer for Salvation:

Lord Jesus I ask you to come into my heart and take my life over. I am a sinner and I need you to save me. I believe that you died on the Cross for me and rose again on the third day to pay the penalty for my sins. Father God, thank you for your Love for me, that you would give your only begotten Son for me. Thank you Father, I love you, thank you for your mercy and grace...In Jesus name...Amen.

attend to my words; *Proverbs 4:19-21*-***note page***

attend to my words; *Proverbs 4:19-21*-**note page**

Established in Peace
Peace is more than an Emotion
It is a Kingdom Dominion

Blessed are the peacemakers: for they shall be called the children of God. **Matthew 5:9**

Peace is the greatest neutralizer of WAR, whether it be mental, emotional, spiritual or conventional warfare. As we stated earlier, our Lord Jesus Christ has a WAR garment, it is a "Vesture dipped in Blood". This scripture in Rev 19:13 personifies our Lord Jesus Christ in one of his many roles and offices... He is here depicted as God of the Angel armies in Rev 19:14. In another Scripture he is called the Prince of Peace:

...and his name shall be called...The Prince of Peace. **Isaiah 9:6**

Jesus is the Commander of Peace, he has dominion over it in every way. He demonstrated this by commanding Peace to stop the winds in **Mark 4:39.** The on looking religious leaders thought that he commanded the winds, but he actually commanded Peace. This is a Kingdom Dominion. This Kingdom Dominion is living inside of every believer in a measure.

*For the kingdom of God is not meat and drink; but righteousness, **and peace**, and joy in the Holy Ghost.* **Romans 14:17**

Peace, as a Kingdom Dominion, has a tremendous influence on our emotions. This Peace comes as a supernatural manifestation from God to subdue all rebellion and opposition, and to bring all things into submission to it's dominion voluntarily. It literally neutralizes WAR. I have walked in this peace that passes all understanding for seasons in my life where my every faculty was at REST. The phenomenon was so amazing that it appeared as if time itself had slowed to half pace.

This Peace has nothing to do with weakness or surrender. It imposes it's will with precision of rule. Jesus, the Warrior King of Glory is also the Prince of Peace.

PRAYER:

I declare the Dominion of Peace be unto you now in the name of our Lord and Savior Jesus Christ. I release unto you the Rest of our Lord and Savior Jesus Christ. Receive the dominion of Rest!

SAY THIS WITH ME: I receive the Rest of the Lord Jesus Christ. I receive the Peace of the Lord Jesus Christ. Yes, I receive the Dominion of Peace.

You are now established in Peace. Pray this as often as you need to, it will reinforce this Kingdom Dominion of Peace in your life. As this Dominion is manifested in you...Go and be a Peacemaker!

Concluding thoughts

- Maintain readiness

- Refuse the Gall

- Refuse Dominating Emotions

- Preserve your internal environment

- Review the principles until they are living realities

- Continue steadfastly in prayer

- Declare freedom from harmful life events

- Declare Freedom from past traumas

- Make these truths your daily declarations

    A) I have a Kingdom Fortified Mind
    B) I am covered in a vesture dipped in blood
    C) No Imaginations
    D) Love dominates me
    E) I am established in Peace

attend to my words; <u>Proverbs 4:19-21</u>*-note page*

attend to my words; <u>Proverbs 4:19-21</u>**-note page**

Other Published Books By Richard Taylor

- **A Beauty Mark: The Mark of an Overcomer**
  On Amazon.com & Barnesandnoble.com In paperback and kindle editions...Available for order at your local bookstore.

Upcoming Books

- **The Five-Fold Spiritual Power of Humility**

Acknowledgements:

Special thanks to my wife Estelle, my chief intercessor, woman of faith and best friend; to my Spiritual Mentor's over the past 25 years: Wade Taylor, Jay Francis, Matthew Caruso, Herbert Rylander and other great men and women of God who played a significant role in my life; to Denise Courts, Tony Flood and Brett Tomkins for spiritual seasonings; to Basil and Roxann Robinson for apostolic impartations; to the Master's Table family for your love and support; to Richard Taylor Sr., Barney Christie, Anthony Christie, and to my mother Joyce Christie-Taylor for a mother's love, and the gift of writing; to my children (natural and spiritual sons and daughters) and grandchildren, I release a generational blessing of spiritual life... Above all I thank my Heavenly Father for the gift of His Son Jesus Christ, my Lord and Savior, and the presence of The Holy Spirit within my life and ministry.

Gall: Overcoming the Power of Dominating Emotions
By Richard Taylor

For
Ministry Bookings/Itinerary
Speaking Engagements/
Author Events/
Book Signings/
Call 860-206-0424
Author Website:

Ministry Affiliation
The Master's Table Ministries
Pastor Richard Taylor
(Senior Pastor)

P.O. Box 290290
Wethersfield, CT
(860) 904-2768
www.themasterslove.org

Made in the USA
Charleston, SC
24 April 2014